PRAISE FOR MARC FLITTER
AND
JUDITH'S PAVILION

"Gripping . . . and deeply moving . . . prose as clean as a neuro-surgeon's work, yet also lyrical and at times beautiful."
        —*Publishers Weekly* (starred review)

"Marc Flitter writes with extraordinary sensitivity and moral reflectiveness. . . . His book is marked by a tender, melancholy realism—the realism unyielding—which is, somehow, genuinely illuminating and even heartening."
        —**Michael Walzer**

"A voice that is convincing, affecting, original, and eloquent . . . so gentle and thoughtful, writing of these people with such skill, compassion, and tenderness, that we mourn them less than we meet them as our fellow human beings."
    —**Robert Coles, M.D.,** *New England Journal of Medicine*

"A sensitively drawn portrait of his own fears and misgivings as he moves through his nerve-wracking career. . . . Flitter [draws] a reader into the harrowing business of trying to perform miracles against the tides of disaster."
        —*Washington Post Book World*

"A collection of beautifully written stories artfully strung together by a fine craftsman. . . . Fans of Richard Selzer will find much to savor here. Flitter's surgical descriptions are filled with lovely images . . . a surprisingly engaging book."
        —*Kirkus Reviews* (starred review)

more . . .

JUDITH'S PAVILION

The Haunting Memories of a Neurosurgeon

MARC FLITTER, M.D.

WARNER BOOKS

A Time Warner Company

WARNER BOOKS EDITION

Copyright © 1997 by Mark Flitter, M.D.
All rights reserved.

This Warner Books edition is published by arrangement with Steerforth Press L.C., P.O. Box 70, South Royalton, VT 05068

Warner Books, Inc., 1271 Avenue of the Americas, New York, NY 10020

Visit our Web site at http://warnerbooks.com

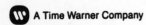 A Time Warner Company

Printed in the United States of America

First Trade Printing: July 1998

10 9 8 7 6 5 4 3 2 1

Library of Congress Cataloging-in-Publication Data

Flitter, Marc.
  Judith's pavilion : the haunting memories of a neurosurgeon / by Marc Flitter.
      p. cm.
  Previously published: South Royalton, Vt. : Steerforth Press, 1997.
  ISBN 0-446-67472-9
  1. Nervous system--Surgery--Miscellanea.   2. Neurosurgeons--Miscellanea.   3. Physician and patient--Miscellanea.   I. Title
RD593.F58 1998
617.4'8--DC21   97-42587
                                                                      CIP

Cover design by Julie Metz
Cover insert photos © Tom Collicott/Graphistock

To my wife, Alice

CONTENTS

PREFACE

In the Marais district of Paris, there is a vocational school with the words ECOLE de TRAVAIL etched in stone above the portal. I asked my wife to photograph me there, standing on the front step as if I were a returning alumnus. Perhaps I sought to add that facade to my curriculum vitae. My undergraduate studies at Lafayette College, medical school at Temple University, and my residency in neurological surgery at Temple University Hospital were but prelude to the education I was to receive from the practice of neurosurgery. Those patients who have remained unforgettable to me should be added to my resumé as well. By telling their stories I did not intend to write a book about how our lives end. If that is the common thread that joins these tales, it is because we do not commission the artist of our memory so much as serve his commanding view. I believe all men gather within themselves a like-minded body of experience. What is remembered from the privileged view of a neurosurgeon may differ only in details to that recalled by a tradesman or artisan. I suspect the themes are the same.

I have attempted to avoid the perils of voyeurism, not only because of my duty to do so by virtue of the Hippocratic oath, but because of my respect for the men and women I came to know. They were strangers who admitted me into their lives in exchange for my acquired skills. Even without the compensation I received it would have been a fair trade, secrets for the stuff of healing. Whatever difference existed between us was temporal. All men suffer their fate.

The names of the patients and those of most of my colleagues have been changed. But Drs. Scott and Murtagh and Buchheit were the professors whose dedication to medicine and teaching allowed me to become a neurosurgeon. The respect and admiration I hold for them continues to grow as I come to see and understand more of what their lives have been all about.

I have not changed the names of institutions. Miami Heart Institute and Mount Sinai Medical Center are the hospitals in which I was granted neurosurgical privileges during my practice in Miami Beach, Florida from 1976 to 1987. Institutions endure. It is the men and women who work in them who must someday leave to be replaced by others with greater skills, proficiency, and knowledge. The moments in time I have described tell less of these institutions than of the frailty of the human beings who inhabited them.

Lastly I would like to thank Alan Lelchuk, my friend and mentor. My gratitude to him can not be simply expressed in an acknowledgment. The creation of this work has been inseparable from him, from its inception to its completion. I have no doubt that on the day I am a last patient, I shall see him from my bed, consulting with my beloved professors.

Our whole life is a dream enveloped in death.

— Walter, in *The Mozart Brothers*

PART ONE

The Pavilion

FAMILIARITY

Judith Halpern and her husband, Ben, sat across from my desk as if they had been sent to the principal's office and didn't know why. As retirees to Miami Beach, they made an unlikely truant couple. Judith's silver hair, like that of most of her friends, bordered on blue and offered no hint of the brown shoulder-length locks that at her wedding had inspired envy of the beaming groom. Her hands that gripped the armrests of her chair were spotted — periods to the concluded sentences of her life, the children grown, the business prospered and finally sold, the myriad redecorations of their home of which she finally tired. But her eyes still merited contemplation of reprimand. They burned as they had when she was her husband's high school sweetheart. She used them now as her last unweathered resource. There was a girl behind that grandmother's face, an ageless spirit now called to task.

Her husband seemed defeated. He was slumped in depression as if he were the patient facing a surgery he knew would be too much. It was not only because of the difference in their age. His six years' seniority was just about the average for most of their friends and helped explain why all the husbands were dying first. His prop was being taken away, the hand at his arm when he needed to negotiate the three steps from the patio to the pool, the valet, who always made sure that his collar was turned over his tie. His companion, who had delicately shaved the hair on his ears, could no longer button her own blouse. If Ben's memory were failing it was simply because he had entrusted it to Judith, never thinking he might someday forget to ask for its return. His leathered face seemed more taxidermic than rejuvenated. He looked at the floor as if considering that he might just as well become a fixture there. Never leave, never go forward with what they both now feared.

I held Judith's CAT scan against the light from the ceiling-to-floor windows to the left of my desk. I could see the time and temperature sign on the roof of the department store across the street. Beyond it the sun reflected on the ocean off Miami Beach. On days when my practice seemed an endless succession of arthritic spines or traumatic sprains that my patients hoped would become legal bonanzas, I would stare through the films in my hand at the freighters that passed by on the Gulf Stream horizon and transport myself to those great ships and their crews. But I had neither the need nor the desire to be absent from these two. They had my full attention. This was what I was all about, what I had wanted to become since I was thirteen and had read *Death Be Not Proud,* by John Gunther, the story of his son who had died of a malignant brain tumor, the type of tumor I thought that Judith had.

I would have preferred she had a different kind. Instead of the dark presence hiding below her cortical surface, I would have chosen a stand-out freak, something with angry blood vessels coursing through an irregular surface like the pock-marked face of some convenience-store bandit. Six years into my neurosurgical practice I knew how to deal with a come-and-get-me maniac like that, a tumor that thought just because it had grown around a few cranial nerves and a crucial artery that it was safe. Separate it from normal tissue and I could almost hear, "Don't come any closer or the old lady's a goner."

I could direct the anesthesiologist to slip the patient some mannitol, a drug that caused a normal brain to shrink, drawing it away from the tumor. Retractors could be placed at the hint of a margin as if a window with a view of some storefront hostage drama were being pried open. The operating microscope would offer a sniper's view of both perpetrator and victim. The orange spotting beam of the laser could be aimed at portions of tumor clearly remote from surrounding brain. The imagined lunatic could be vaporized then until all that remained were the equivalent of shoes and a cap. The final dissection to free the hostage would be a piece of cake.

But calling to me from the films in my hand, was a different kind of psychopath, the type of tumor that buried itself within the brain and merged imperceptibly with normal tissue. It would grow silently, gradually taking up more space until it was ready to declare itself. When a patient like Judith began to fall or drag one leg, leading to some inquiries, it would continue to remain elusive. Even after luring patient and surgeon to the operating room, it would seem petulant, withdrawing further into surrounding tissue, obscuring the border between normal and deadly. If the report of the biopsy specimen, hand-carried to the lab, was "You've got a highly malignant neoplasm here," the tumor would crow its approval. Although nothing would delight it more, than the subtle accusation of the surgeon being in the wrong place, "This looks like normal tissue, maybe just a little increased cellularity, but nothing we can call." And it would always want to have the last say,

"Radiation and chemotherapy are the only hope," or, "Perhaps it's best just to get the patient home for whatever time is left." That's the kind of tumor I thought that Judith Halpern had.

My rapport with Judith extended beyond just a clinical challenge. If she and her husband didn't live in the same condominium building that my mother had moved to five years earlier, they were close enough. I knew about their lives, their morning exercise classes, and their cronies by the pool. I winced at their opening the can of tuna that they shared with tea and lemon for lunch. I had heard about their conversations during afternoon canasta in the card room and could see them waiting in the Early Bird Special line outside a restaurant on Collins Avenue. They were "lifers," members of the fifty-year and plus club. Their portrait might have easily been included in the *Family of Man,* the "We Two Are One" section. It wasn't because of what the South Florida sun had done to their skin, or a "gold on gold" appearance, as the thinly veiled anti-Semite who was once my colleague was fond of saying. The lines in their faces told the same story, recorded the same history, revealed their accomplishments and failures. Judith and Ben related her history in recitative comfort, completing each other's sentences with the certainty of practiced narrative.

Judith's headaches had been increasing over the past three months. One week before her visit she had fallen in their apartment and had struck the corner of her eye on an end table, the one with the porcelain birds. Two flew over the side onto the carpet below.

"Thank God they didn't break," was what she had said.

She had seen her internist then. He asked her to do some simple things, touch her nose, walk across the room, one foot in front of the other, just as if she had been stopped by a state trooper and had to prove she hadn't been drinking. Ben laughed at that, "his Judith," who barely had a sip of wine on the holidays. But then she couldn't do it, couldn't walk that straight line, heel to toe, without help, without the internist steadying her, holding her full-fleshed upper arm, that she preferred keeping covered. He ordered a CAT scan and referred her to me after the radiologist called him with the results. There was an area in the cerebellum, the back portion of the brain that controls coordination and balance, that was "suspicious." There was a possibility it was a tumor.

Her examination was abnormal. Her balance had deteriorated even more in the week since she had been to the internist. The films showed why. There was something in just the right place, the correct side and location in her brain, to explain her symptoms. It fell upon me to describe what lay ahead.

Above all I wanted to leave them hope. I had read the books that offered the tenets of medical ethics. They suggested that any distortion of the truth was wrong. Practicing as a neurosurgeon, I had found that the truth was elusive, subject to unknowable events which had to play themselves out before the destiny of any one patient was immutably set. What earthly good would it have served to share with them at the very beginning my darkest prediction of her future? We were three human beings in a room with the trappings of a profession, physician with patient and spouse, the practiced with the unfamiliar. I was not some clairvoyant they had consulted in an effort to interpret the mounting signs of impending ruin. I was the embodiment of short-term salvation, if that were available. And if it is true that physicians treat themselves, or at least should try, then what I presented to them made sense to me, was what I would have wished to hear had fate placed me in that dreaded leather chair.

The first hope I extended to her, as if offering individual flowers from a bouquet, was the hope of a sanguine diagnosis. Occasionally the interpretation of a CAT scan was incorrect.

Images on a film were not histologic proof of a tumor. Stroke and infection could mimic in appearance the stain of a tumor within the brain. Why not such a salutary finding for her? That it was rare, was undeniable.

Next I offered the possibility of cure, that if it were a "growth," perhaps it could be entirely removed, phrased as if I had handed her not one, but two delicate stems. "Growth" was a term suggesting she might not have cancer, and "cure" would be recalled from her first conscious nursery, a hurt set right. Lastly, perhaps with just the slightest admonition — *Be sure they're kept in water with plenty of light* — I suggested the possibility of effective treatment, a coexistent truce, completing the best that I could offer. I explained that if it were a "growth" that could not be completely removed, we might recommend radiation or chemotherapy to "control" any cells that might be left behind. Hope first, but afterward a plan, alternatives, a choice that they must make, that Judith must live with.

Finally, I assumed the role of architect to her commissioned frame of reference. "If this problem inside your brain were something that we felt could be left alone for the time being," I reasoned aloud, "perhaps simply followed with serial scans, that would be my recommendation. But your difficulty with balance and your increasing headaches, along with what we see on the CAT scan, makes that seem somewhat unreasonable. There's always the risk of your falling and breaking a hip. If this condition turns out to be something that we can remove or that is treatable it would be preferable not to delay."

It was what she had thought about in the days before her appointment. Perhaps if they had been shopping for drapes or listening to a salesman's pitch about additional health care insurance, three hundred and sixty days of nursing home coverage, she would have turned to her husband and deferred to his role as the first to answer. Now, hope aside — she had heard enough from the internist to understand why she was being sent to a neurosurgeon — she spoke for herself. Perhaps she was starting to say good-bye to the companion at her side.

"The headaches are better since I started taking the medicine my doctor prescribed. But the dizziness and falling haven't improved much. I'd like you to go ahead and schedule the surgery."

Ben didn't look up, whether it was from relief that she had spoken or simply not wanting to show his fear. "Yes, I agree," was his faint addition.

They hadn't waited for me to talk about risks, or explain exactly what I would be doing. There was a resignation to their decision, as if it didn't matter, there was no other choice. In part it was the surroundings in which they lived, like being back in school. But the curriculum in their retirement community was not of their choice. It consisted of watching their peers graduate from life. Their youngest friend, Bertie — they had often wondered why she lived in their building — was found dead by the doorman who called each morning for a tenant check.

"Massive stroke," was all they heard.

The couple with whom they had gone to dinner each Saturday night died within six months of each other — the husband from a heart attack in the pool on a July afternoon, the wife while visiting her daughter in Columbus. They never learned exactly what had happened to her. One of their friends was confined to his apartment because of his progressive Parkinson's disease. It sounded to them as if a guard had been stationed at his door. Parkinson, Pinkerton, it didn't matter. If he fell out of bed after the woman who was with him from nine to five had left, he would simply lay there until the next morning.

It wasn't as if the healthy ones sat around waiting, or rushed about like passengers on the *Ship of Fools,* ignorant of the coming carnage. It simply meant that they were perhaps somewhat less startled by a knocking on their stateroom door than they might otherwise have been. That's what Judith's fall and dizziness and the report of the CAT scan seemed to be, someone or something at the door. No use not to open up. Can't see anything through the peephole. And while she and Ben stood there without moving, hardly breathing, a note was pushed underneath their door. Maybe it was my business card with the date and the time that now flashed on the roof outside my office window.

It was time to let them know what I would be doing. Not everything, not every last detail that might haunt their imaginations between this office visit and the operating room, but enough so that they would understand that she faced some risks. Informed consent carried more than a legal obligation. It was the common decency to tell Judith where we both were going.

The operative exposure was to be through the portion of Judith's skull between and below her ears. She would need to be placed in the sitting position. I didn't make that a part of the discussion, explain how she would be held partially erect in a Mayfield head holder, three pins through her scalp and into her skull. The device never failed to evoke an image in my mind. It was that of a fatal car accident. The driver's seat had buckled from the impact, forcing the backrest to an inclined position. But the victim was found looking straight ahead, as if he were still driving or trying to see what was coming across the median out of an impenetrable fog. He was held in that position by what seemed to be a headband attached to the rearview mirror. Not that there was enough metal and glass to encircle his head completely, just enough from ear to ear and between his eyes to hold his attention. That's what the medical examiner's slide seemed to show, the one he would place at the beginning of his carousel projector. It didn't matter if he were speaking to a hospital staff meeting or to a Howard Johnson's gathering of the Kiwanis club. He would point out the metal that seemed to be merging with that victim's head in three places, a three-point fixation. And there was a second slide, a dream maker. It was taken after a fireman with the "jaws of life" ended up extracting the victim in two parts. Maybe that's why I stopped explaining the "semi-sitting position." I wanted to think of Judith Halpern as whole, going in and coming out.

It was the first of my editorial judgments. I'd decide what they had to know. If I listed everything that could go wrong, we'd be there all day, or she might break. Run out of the office as if bolting from a dentist's chair, out of a semi-sitting position.

I omitted as well the report of the patient whose head holder was tightened too much. The pins kept going. Penetrated the skull and the covering of the brain before they stopped. At the end of the case there was weeping where the pins had been, spinal fluid running down the patient's face in mournful protest. And even if the pins were fixed in the proper place, anchored into her skull with the appropriate force, there was still a chance of infection, and not simply of her scalp. It could spread to surrounding bone, the bacteria welcome there, free to stay as long as they liked. Antibiotic treatment might not dislodge them. More surgery would be necessary to remove the infected part of her skull. That would leave a hole in the bone underneath her scalp. "Cosmetic significance only" is how I would have concluded that detail. Even that would not have been entirely true. I had cared for a patient who had been stabbed in the brain through such a portal. His "soft spot" was not just an eyesore. A penknife had been plunged through that pulsating target by a "friend" in a North Philadelphia bar. The assailant might have thought about that spot for months, watched it ticking away with each beat of the heart, until the night a friendship turned to murderous rage. It seemed the natural thing to do then, plunge a knife into that tireless forehead. Perhaps he thought the victim might deflate or that he might hear a tiny cry.

I had been familiar with similar musings, even if not overtly homicidal. It was during my neurosurgical residency. I had become intrigued within my darkest allowable heart with the toupee of a fellow resident. Each time a minor confrontation occurred about scheduling, or who would do which case, my attention was drawn to his bogus hairline. He had a broad forehead and walked as if he were on roller skates, so that to watch him come down a hospital corridor was to have the impression that the toupee was gliding toward me. He spoke with an Illinois resignation, as if he assumed that most of what he said could not be heard above the stockyard din. His eyes were peculiarly motionless, not so much as if he were drugged, but as if the pelt on the top of his head were holding on too tightly. All of this at eye level, like the pulsating forehead of my violated patient. And I had developed a plan. If it ever came to *mano a mano* in the resident's conference room, years of education and career planning asked to wait outside, along with the junior resident and the marquess of Queensberry, his toupee would have been the next to leave, the target of my preemptive strike. So much for cosmetic significance only.

Judith Halpern faced the risk of paralysis and death. What would an extra hole in her head be if she were otherwise unscathed? I chose not to burden her and her husband with details about pins in her scalp and the semi-sitting position. If she were to agree to risk her life why would any lesser threat deter her resolve? It just didn't work that way. I had never heard a patient say, "Doctor, I was willing to have you operate upon my brain with a risk of death, coma and paralysis, but what you said about possibly having a pressure point in my scalp that may take weeks to finally heal over was too much. I think I'll just crawl into a corner and die quietly."

It was as if there were two informed consents. One I articulated to her, and a second that I acknowledged only to myself. There was no absolution to be found in a simple litany of all the dangers she was about to face. A warning before the fact did not bestow immunity from blame for occurrences on either list. A screwup with the head holder, and it wouldn't matter that she knew about it going in. I noted only to myself, "We'll have to watch out for an air embolism." That was a bona-fide nightmare waiting to happen, the most serious risk of the semi-sitting position, and not so remote as to be omitted without hesitation. It was simple physics, hydraulics and manometrics. If one of her scalp veins were cut and remained open while she was in that sitting position, her head above her heart, air might be sucked into an irresisitible vortex within that vein, enough drawn down to her heart and from there to her lungs to cause a fatal blockage of breathing.

In the early days of neurosurgery that was "Son of a bitch" time. A sponge would be packed into the wound, the surgical drapes ripped off, the table straightened and the patient repositioned right side up and head down. All of that in the hope that the air could be kept in the heart until it could be withdrawn through a needle. But I planned to control the bleeding from Judith's muscle and bone. The anesthesiologists would insert a catheter into her heart before we began, just in case I couldn't. It was one more anecdote that Judith and Ben would never hear.

I had spared them the roadside slides and the lessons on pulmonary physiology. But my desk was between us for more reasons than paperwork. We needed to come to an understanding. This was Judith's life, her symptoms, and her possible future as best I could portray it. I could not cross to her side and take her hands like some media evangelist asking for divine intercession. It was surgical interdiction that I was talking about. If my demeanor turned somewhat reserved it was to protect them and me. This was not the pep talk part of getting her better. This was about my being licensed and credentialed and willing to perform surgery on her brain.

There was almost no inflection in my voice.

"There is a risk of infection. The chance of that is about one in four hundred. There can be bleeding in the brain. Usually we are able to prevent that. But there are circumstances when it occurs on a delayed basis. In such cases additional surgery may be required. The part of the brain where this tumor is located controls many vital functions. Damage to structures in this region can result in paralysis or double vision, difficulty with swallowing or breathing, persistent coma, or death. Obviously, we do everything possible to avoid these problems. In my experience I have every reason to think that we can get you through this operation without your being harmed. But these risks are real."

Their expressions didn't change. A litany of medical terms delivered to portray the worst possible result, and barely a response. Neither seemed surprised, as if they had been prepared for what they had heard. Fatigue and resignation had coached them. It was the difference between the young and the elderly.

They had used up their reserves. Events were carrying them along now with the momentum of institutions, their trust in a profession, and the progression of her illness. Hadn't their internist advised them there was no other way? What about Fredrickson? He was supposed to have had a brain tumor. They had watched him deteriorate over six months. At first he walked with a walker. They would see him shuffling in the lobby with a nurse by his side, his head bent forward so that he had to raise his eyes to look at them. They remembered his bemused smile. "This is rough," was all he said. Before his illness he had gone swimming every day, chauffeured the ladies around as if he were twenty years younger. But at his age, twenty years younger was still more than over the hill. A list of horrors was not about to deter them now. The horror had been unleashed weeks ago when Judith had fallen and the porcelain birds had landed upon the carpet. It was a sign, though neither of them talked about it then. Their life had changed and they both knew it. The time for figurines and vases, color schemes and everything in its place was over. That's what losing the sense of balance and constant headaches had done. It wasn't acceptable. One way or the other it had to change.

They had checked up on me as well. They hadn't succeeded in building a million-dollar business together, just the two of them, by believing everybody that came down the pike with a new scheme or solicitous idea. They had been in casual shirts. Put a logo on them that had made them famous. Worth millions when they finally sold out. That's when they had moved to Florida, after all the kids had been married off, except the youngest who still hadn't found himself. They knew that having a brain operation wasn't like getting a cavity filled or having a skin tag cut off. Everyone agreed it was delicate and dangerous and you wanted the best to do it. They had asked around their building. "He operated on Mrs. Steinfeld's back and she says she lives by him. Stopped walking with a walker, only uses a cane now."

"My doctor said he would go to him if he needed an operation."

Their daughter, who lived in Shaker Heights, Ohio, wasn't convinced. I had received a call from her physician a day earlier. I explained that I hadn't seen Mrs. Halpern yet, but based on a note I had received from the internist and the report of the CAT scan it certainly seemed likely we would be offering surgery. It was a collegial conversation and went along with practicing in Miami Beach. Almost all my patients had come from somewhere else. Their children, now adults left behind, were of two types: the next-available-flight contingent would show up no matter what; and the we-want-everything-done-and-keep-us-posted group followed their own predictable pattern as well. Consultation with their hometown physician, with whom they were socially or professionally acquainted, was a common request. Almost always these remote doctors were in favor of the parents remaining in Florida. There may have been a local characteristic to these progeny as well, better not to get involved. According to the Halperns' daughter, her doctor was very impressed. It sounded to him as if there were no need for her mother to return to Ohio. Which of course Judith and Ben were prepared to do. They had thought about it, even mentioned that possibility to their friends. They had contributed to the renovation of the children's ward in their hospital. There was a plaque on the wall with their names on it. But they didn't want to delay the surgery.

Judith simply asked, how soon could she have it done? I said I would try to add her to the surgical schedule within the next few days, and then I offered my alternative to the complications I had been obliged to share with them. "We'll take good care of you." It was to reassure myself as much as her. It was to bring us all back from the contemplation of her death and destruction, and to retrieve me from the side of the road by the wreckage of a fatal accident, to extricate me from a pulmonary artery with no way out.

"We'll take good care of you," the words spell-breaking in themselves, like the knocking at the gate in *Macbeth*. If the "we" were royal as well as editorial then so be it. This was about trying to get her better and if that were not possible then for Christ's sake not hurting her.

FAILURE

Judith's surgery was to be done three days after I had seen her in the office. That was enough time for two of her three children to fly to Miami to help her get through it. It was what kids were for, she and her husband agreed. All of us would have preferred if I could have started first thing in the morning, but since she had been added to the schedule we needed to wait for an available operating room. At four in the afternoon, she hugged her family in the holding area, embarrassed about not having her dentures. She hadn't been without makeup in public since who knew when? She looked frail to them as the orderly wheeled her away.

"Come to think of it, maybe this has been going on for the last three months," her husband admitted. "She had to steady herself against the car when we came home from the movies. She fell asleep in one, never did that before."

The daughter had been more worried about her father, older by six years. But the heart medicine that he was taking seemed to be working fine. He still golfed twice a week. "Sharp as ever," was what she told her friends, although she hadn't actually seen him in the last two years. "Let's face it," she philosophized, "none of us is getting younger. Sis needed a hysterectomy just last year."

I placed Judith in the Mayfield head rest and positioned her in that driver's seat. I shaved her hair from the crown of her head to the nape of her neck with electric clippers. For the fine cut, I used an old-fashioned straight razor, the scraping of blade against scalp barely audible above the rhythmic breathing of the ventilator and the measured pulse of her EKG. I nicked her skin in a few places. But the bleeding wasn't enough that the anesthesiologist might quip, "How many units do you have her typed and crossed for?"

Sterile drapes were placed over her head and back so that the only part of Judith Halpern that could still be seen was her shaved scalp and the upper part of her neck. It was as if the rest of her had been excused. I would call her back when it was all over. I didn't want to be forcing my attentions with scalpel and drill on a wife and mother. It was a tumor I was after. The operating room table on which the instruments lay was positioned to almost touch the top of her forehead. What more was she seeing under that table in her sleep of anesthesia than the driver on that medical examiner's slide had seen in his dreamless and timeless sleep?

The edges of the drapes were sutured to her skin to keep them from sagging under the weight of blood and saline irrigation that would heavy them during the case. With scalpel in hand I announced, "We're starting," asserting that declaration beyond the need of the anesthesiologist to note the hour and minute at hand. It was "follow me" to the scrub and circulating nurses. It was convocation, benediction, and grace, stated as economically as I could.

I made what was called a hockey-stick incision. The scalpel traced upward through her skin like a flare at sea, lighting her scalp with its trail of blood. It began at the level of her earlobe and reached its apogee in the midline, its ascent no higher than the occipital protuberance, that bony outcrop on the back of her skull. From there it fell, inscribing the shaft of that pointed constellation to the handle resting in the nape of her neck. Her scalp was thick. A few of the arteries that had been cut sprayed on my gown, and one reached the right lens of my glasses as if I were on the Odessa steps in *The Battleship Potemkin*. Most of the bleeding stopped when I spread the wound edges with a self-retaining retractor, the claw-like ends of that instrument burying themselves in the yellowish subcutaneous tissue. A few vascular holdouts, persistent fireboat celebrants, were extinguished with electric cautery. Then all was still. Her head remained motionless in a three-pinned embrace. There were no veins gulping air.

The part of her skull that lay gleaming under the operating room lights seemed to be taunting, "Get inside if you can." That challenge had been more formidable when neurosurgeons had no power tools, when arm-numbing exertion was required just to drill the first burr hole. I imagined that bone stunned to hear the whine of the pneumatic bit. I enlarged the nickel-sized hole it had produced with biting instruments called rongeurs. Their dinosaur-like jaws tore away at the margins of the skull. I covered the vascular channels in the bone with an occlusive wax, keeping them free of air and the anesthesiologist content. Gradually, as if I were uncovering some buried vase, the rounded outline of the dura, the membranous covering of the brain, appeared. Then it was precision time, the paradox of the exposure. After having broken through the equivalent of a vault, what would be required of me now was the delicacy of repairing a watch or inscribing the Lord's Prayer on a grain of rice.

I changed what I was seeing then, positioned the operating microscope. Its two eyepieces and the objective lens were covered with a transparent sterile drape, all suspended on the end of a three-jointed arm supported on a pedestal. It would be the key to gaining entry to her world. It magnified the wound so that my entire visual field was no wider than the word "eye." Each individual blood vessel, each single fiber of tissue became the object of attention, determining sequential efforts. Distance was traversed in millimeters rather than inches. Even the sounds in the operating room were muted by that view, as if hearing were partly visual. I began to open the dura, using a more delicate scalpel than the one that had violated her skin. It was the transition from dinosaur jaws to jeweler's forceps, from rending to teasing. I held either side of the taut membrane open with a suture that almost whispered its fragile tension, "five-O nylon." It wasn't the smallest suture available, but fine enough to seem as if its strand might easily float away.

I resisted the urge to announce, "let the real operation begin." Held back in part because of what I was seeing. My view was as breathless as if I had reached the summit of Kilimanjaro, or K2, or wherever I had hoped to find an answer. It was brain tissue, the reason why I had kept at it for all those years. Each time a surgical exposure was completed, it was the brain that was revealed. It wasn't the rolls of sausage or a bellyful of eels that the general surgeons ran their fingers along, hoping to find a perforation and subconsciously boasting, "Look how long mine is." It wasn't the speculumed mystery of creation into which the gynecologists peered, seeking contentment. Who knows how they dissipated the memory of exudates? And it wasn't the erector set challenge of long bones and joints that kept the orthopedic surgeons with one foot in a hardware department next to a display of red tool chests. I chose not to think about what the ophthalmologists saw. In neurosurgery it was always the same. It was Stanley coming upon Livingston, and Holmes declaring, "Watson, have a look at this." It was the brain and there was nothing like it. Nothing could replace it. It didn't regenerate. It couldn't be sutured or glued, anastomosed or fused. It was the palpable paradox of Eurydice. To touch it was to lose it in almost all circumstances. The only saving grace of a brain operation was that what remained had such extraordinary potential. That is what I saw through that microscope; magnified, illuminated and waiting.

I touched the surface of Judith's brain, a single cortical gyrus, and it pushed back. Not overwhelmingly, not with the self-assured challenge of the skull, but with enough resistance to convince me that there were secrets to be learned, inscribed in some cerebral Braille. I stroked that same surface with a fine scalpel, just tickling, as if it had a sense of humor, though this was no laughing matter. Bleeding from surface arteries was not the problem. That was dismissed with applications of electrical current between the two ends of a bipolar forceps. But the paste-like appearance of whitish brain tissue signaled a loss that all the king's men could not put back inside. Only a fool could fail to read that message. No inconsequential steps were to be taken here. To proceed was at the risk of worlds.

But I was not there through chance trespass. My warranted search for the cause of Judith's imbalance had led me to that place. I had divined from the CAT scan that two inches below the surface of her brain lay the root of her dysfunction. I inserted the cup-like ends of a biopsy forceps through the cortical incision. The instrument was pistol gripped. Squeezing the trigger closed the tissue-gathering ends within the brain. I fired then and watched the approximated tip's retreat. There was no sense of tearing as if some tenacious artery had become enraged. I saw no angry surge of blood that welled behind the silver instrument. Through the dissolute cortical incision, all was quiet.

I deposited the contents upon a waiting sponge and instructed the circulating nurse, "Send this for frozen section. Label it brain tumor."

I offered saline irrigation to the violated surface while we waited for the pathologist's answer. As I watched, the exposed portion of the brain began to undergo a transformation. It seemed that something was being offered to me, neither sought nor desired. Brain tissue was being forced through the confines of the exposure. The implication was that there was bleeding at the biopsy site, that a clot was forming, pushing tissue ahead of it. I inserted retractors along the stained path that had marked the passage of the biopsy forceps. At the apparent site from which I had harvested the specimen, a gray and yellow discoloration of the normal brain reinforced the suspicion of tumor. The metallic voice of the pathologist confirmed the diagnosis on the speaker phone, dispassionately announcing in deadly alliteration, "anaplastic astrocytoma." But diagnosis was no longer the problem. There was no clot that I could see and yet the tissue kept coming, extruding like lava without apparent end.

It was one of those moments that can occur during an operation that is defined by alarm. There was a visceral sense of being swept away, as if the malevolent force unleashed upon Judith had reached out and taken hold of me as well. Any hope of regaining mastery lay first in conceptual insight. What was the problem? Since I had not encountered blood along that biopsy track, only the concept of malignant brain edema offered a possible explanation. It was an alternative that begged exoneration. It wasn't I, not the surgeon who brought her into that room, placed her in the semi-sitting position, opened the base of her skull, and cut into her brain for a bit of tissue. It was someone or something else, inside.

Whether it was true or not, at least I had an enemy I could engage. Medication was called for, a drug that might spirit away the edema fluid that was causing the tissue to expand to twice its normal size. But that remedy had no effect on her, not that afternoon turning into night.

I took a different tack then, thinking there had to be bleeding. I just wasn't seeing it. I began to look beyond the site of the biopsy, deeper within the tumor. It was a mission of search and destroy. There was no environmentally safe journey into that forest. I might just as well have gone in with heavy equipment. There was bleeding then, and from more than one site. I was drawn further into the magnified world of the microscope. The blood might just as well have been descending upon a sleeping town, avalanche or mud slide, it made no difference. It carried the familiar and the recognizable with it, but somehow all wrong. Fragments of brain, cortex and white matter, welled up in that bleeding like victims being swept past in a torrent. They made their own brief appearance as if in protest or farewell and then were lost in the swell of the rising blood, which could not be stopped so much as hidden beneath strips of cotton. Was this what I had referred to only three days before in my office, with a view of the time and temperature and the gliding ships beyond, when I had said there can be bleeding in the brain?

I went through the motions of a final effort, widened the bony exposure and extended the dural opening. All that did was to invite more brain to escape forever its normal confines. Finally her body's coagulation abilities, the counter-pressure of cotton paddies, and her falling blood pressure stemmed the flow. By then it was too late. Underneath those paddies lay a quiet pool of ruin and devastation that could not be undone. There was no need to wait until the morning to assess the damage. The patient would not survive. I had seen this before, in my own cases and those of my colleagues and professors.

Then, almost unannounced — I certainly hadn't sent for her — Judith returned to the room. It wasn't just a small opening in sterile drapes through which brain tissue had herniated that was my charge. A human being lay there, now irreversibly lost. She was not bionic woman, to be made as good as new with a prosthesis and rehabilitation. She was mother and wife undone, as removed from the world of her family as if she had died last year and had been buried back in Ohio. And it wasn't just the silver-haired retiree who had asked, "When can you schedule it?" who had returned. A handsome woman who was the president of her Temple sisterhood was there. The sweatered bride, the wife of the boss who filled in as secretary and who was secretly watched by all the workers, stood by the wall, one of her seamed-stockinged legs bent casually at the knee. The aproned mother whom her family had seen coming through doorways with dishes that seemed as if they had been cooking all day, the tzimmes and the kugel, the flaishik that she made with those baby browned potatoes, entered too. She was white on white, no longer flushed with the soup. I was outnumbered, even before I had completed the closure and made my way to her waiting family.

APPRENTICESHIP

They didn't teach failure in medical school, how to tell a husband and children their wife and mother is no more. It had to sink in along the way, proportionate to the responsibility assumed for patients' lives, how a physician could become an agent of ruin and death. The apprenticeship of my residency steeled me for such an inevitability. Dr. Scott, my benevolent professor of neurosurgery, served as my mentor for disaster as well as healing. His penchant for euphemism seemed to support him through his most trying cases. He taught us how to save ourselves when the outcome was not what we would have wished it to be. I recounted along with the other residents his more memorable phrases as an example of his endearing eccentricity. I didn't know then I was to become whom I mimicked. But it was Dr. Scott who was to serve as my guide when I spoke to Judith Halpern's family the night of her surgery. The "situation" of her breathing, and her hoped-for "status" in the morning were phrases that would diffuse the awful truth of her imminent death. Otherwise how might we communicate in the face of tragedy, short of collective wailing?

It all came down to "factors." "Very good, but there's a little factor there." That's what Dr. Scott had said, with the patient still awake, and the Xray showing that the spinal needle had transfixed the usually untouchable brain stem, that most primitive part of the brain entrusted with the will to breathe. This occurred in the radiology department at Temple University Hospital before CAT scans or MRIs allowed insurance clerks to diagnose brain tumors. Patients needed to be violated then, to have contrast material injected into an artery or a spinal fluid space so that the anatomy of the brain could be seen on Xray. Chemkowski was the patient, positioned on a straight-back wooden chair, barely minus the leather restraints. His head was flexed so that his chin almost touched his chest. "Try to remain still," was the advice of one of the residents. It was a request for cooperation. After all, this was something between surgeon and tumor. If Chemkowski could have stayed in his room, just sent the tumor down for the test, it would have been preferred. But he and his tumor were like Siamese twins joined at the head. They never went anywhere apart. "OK, you can come," was the reluctant arrangement. That was the attitude of the observing residents. Dr. Scott had assumed the airs of a maitre d' at a linened restaurant, even if he fell somewhat short of looking the part. His stature was more suited for custom fitting than gliding between tables. His eyes were partially obscured by his silver-rimmed glasses. It was the measure of the man that whomever he addressed perceived themselves as his sole object of interest. His gray hair was parted in the middle, leaving no doubt as to the unwavering fairness with which he accomplished his administrative duties. There was a perpetual corner to his mouth, as if he had just finished, or were about to deliver, a sympathetic aside. Whatever he did say was suitable for transcription, which was in fact one of his teaching techniques. On our daily rounds, he would stand by the nurses' desk on a hospital floor while his current resident, a graduate physician, in many instances a husband and father, dutifully recorded the daily progress note. No wonder all of our progress notes eventually read the same. This was the neurosurgeon who had ushered Chemkowski to that inquisitional chair as if the finest of meals was about to be served.

Dr. Scott had done a cisternal tap, had guided a spinal needle between the base of Chemkowski's skull and the uppermost part of the spine. While waiting for the Xray that would confirm the location of that needle, Dr. Scott searched the inside of his cheek with the tip of his tongue. It was his way of marking time. The intervals of his patience were marked by a reassuring word, "Fine," or "Very good." There was not the least change in that melodic voice when the Xray technician returned with the film and snapped it into the wall-mounted viewing box.

It could have been, even to the initiated, the face of Medusa. The details of the base of the skull seemed quite normal. There was no problem there. Instead the needle seemed to be penetrating time itself. It was the kind of suspension that occurs in a dream. A surgeon might see himself once again as a ninth-grade biology student who has just rendered his laboratory frog suitable for dissection. But between the open sides of Chemkowski's white gown, instead of green, rough reptilian edges, there was skin. And even more remarkable, was his unscathed animus, his even respirations. "Are we almost done?" came his not unreasonable sigh. Dr. Scott's response, which was to become for the next decade our training program's, "Don't give up the ship," was his perfectly metered, "Fine, very good," adding as he withdrew the needle with the flair of a matador, "but there's a little factor there."

"Factor," that's what it was going to be when we would have to talk to patients and their families about real nightmares. If the patient and surgeon were fortunate — "better to be lucky than smart," as Kelleher, our chief resident would say — it would become nothing more than an anecdote, an uneventful silver needle transfixing the brain stem.

But luck sometimes ran out, and we all knew it. Nelson Graves had been stricken with multiple sclerosis in his thirties and rendered a house-bound invalid by his varied symptoms. And yet there was to be no barring of the gates to further suffering. He had developed a condition of facial pain that pursued him from room to room. It peered over his shoulder, knife poised, as he brushed his teeth. It stationed itself behind his dining room chair at meal times and utensiled each swallow with a slashing penalty. He was ultimately referred to Dr. Scott for an injection of absolute alcohol into the trigeminal ganglion, the nerve structure responsible for his pain. It was a procedure that had the potential to deliver Graves from his unrelenting tormentor.

As the procedure began, Graves barely flinched as Dr. Scott punctured the skin of the cheek an inch beyond the corner of his thin lips. It seemed to make him sneer at the proceedings. But the unerring course of that needle beneath the skin hardly merited scorn. Dr. Scott had guided the tip unseen through the foramen ovale, an opening in the base of the skull. Grave's sneer turned to a tethered grimace when the target was impaled. Patient and doctor were almost home free. Except there was a "factor." Somehow the injected alcohol leaked outside the confines of the target, out of the Gasserian ganglion, and spilled into a nearby spinal fluid space. It cascaded along there like a maddened vandal destroying whatever it bathed. And in its wake, Graves, with textbook authenticity, presented a parade-like review of cranial nerve dysfunction. His unaffected side served as a control to that "factor." In Graves' search for relief of pain, he had been transformed into a two-faced rendition of one of our first neuroanatomy lectures and his wretchedness was absolute.

Half of his face was analgesic, absent of sensation. Of all his complications, this was the least undesirable, for his pain had been relieved. But the total loss of sensation had extended to his cornea, the surface of his eye. In combination with the acquired paralysis of the muscles responsible for closing his eyelid, that eye had been made vulnerable to ulceration. He would not feel whatever might alight upon that transparent surface. There could be no reflex blinking of the eye initiated by an alien particle until it could be swept aside. Since any ulceration of that surface could lead to scarring and permanent visual loss, Graves' eye was patched, his vision blocked, liberty deprived under martial law. The patch kept hidden another consequence of that destructive spill. The nerve that had turned his eye outward could do so no more. The "treatment" for such limitation had already been applied, a patch which prevented Graves from experiencing double vision in the disrupted synchrony of that ocular motor paralysis.

Other of his symptoms were beyond patching, could not be covered up in symbolic white gauze. Because half of his face was paralyzed, there was a gravity-induced asymmetry to his appearance. It was as if some sinister force, reaching from his future grave, had grabbed him by that face. It seemed to tighten its grip each time he attempted to swallow or speak. His voice was muted and indistinct as if he were already speaking from that final destination. His shoulders tilted, so that in his tortured pacing of the corridor, he seemed like Quasimodo.

Graves remained in the hospital for several weeks, became a fixture of our unintended effort. He was a walking advertisement for our department. There had been others. There was Henning, the executive who had been in charge of a hundred employees, who was wheelchair-bound and seemingly retarded after suffering a hemorrhagic stroke. For some reason the nurses always stationed him by the elevator. Each time the doors opened he would announce the Kurtz of his vocabulary, a guttural "buck" followed by a pause, then "height." He repeated those two syllables of his surgeon's name in a whispered, stepping cadence. The guttural "buck" ended on a hopeful note, only to be paradoxically dashed in the descending resignation of "height."

"Buccheit, Buccheit."

I wondered what the other patients thought as they heard that unanswerable page. Perhaps it made no sense to some, just a garbled version of the wares available on our particular floor. But what about those who had deciphered its meaning, and had seen Graves limping by, a ringing in his ears from his damaged auditory nerve? Surely some of them had contemplated signing out, succumbing to a premonition that there might be nothing left behind of them but dental records.

It wasn't just other patients who may have been unnerved by Henning and Graves. Both had impressed upon me the notion to firstly, do no harm. They had made me a believer of what Kelleher uttered between drags on his cigarette, his eyes narrowing to avoid the smoke, "Listen, if they die without surgery, it's God's will. If we operate on them and they die, we're the one's who knocked them off." Henning and Graves converted me to that old-time religion.

Even the most fervid disciple can fall. There are "factors" inherent in surgery that are as varied as each patient. Who would have thought that Judith would have developed fatal brain swelling from what started out as a straightforward biopsy? To rationalize that it was a "factor" was not so much an excuse, as a refuge. I might just as well have chosen a military metaphor, considered her a casualty of war and manifested a preference for declaration over euphemism. I had precedent for that as well.

Fred Murtagh was second in command to Dr. Scott at the beginning of my residency. It was 1970, and V-J Day was twenty-five years in the past but it seemed as if Murtagh were still stationed somewhere in the Pacific. His black hair and short sideburns were always trimmed to code. His uniform consisted of khaki pants, brown penny loafers, a white button-down oxford shirt and a regimental tie. Each day he donned a newly cleaned and starched three-quarter length white coat. He had a dimple in his chin that with his fearsome eye-brows formed a triangular insignia. The man was his name, Murtagh, two syllables, the chin before the face, a soldier and a civilian, an officer and a neurosurgeon.

On one occasion in the operating room he ordered one of the residents to go outside and tell the family that the patient was going to die. It was only the first part of his strategy to deal with the uncontrollable bleeding he had encountered. For a short while later he barked to no one in particular, although I suppose he assumed the anesthesiologists were listening, "Mobilize all available blood-stopping mechanisms." Those of us with him that day knew for whom that order was intended. We knew he was back on the deck of a battleship and that whether from a kamikaze run, or a torpedo, the ship and its crew had been hit. He had alluded to such an event on other occasions and had described the days of non-stop surgery that had followed. In a way he had never left there, had refused to abandon that high point of his life. He was my captain of the *Caine,* with a battle-earned reason for his defensive reaction to stress. No amount of strawberry episodes could change that he had in fact been off Okinawa while I was still in diapers, and he was performing neurosurgery on the home front while I was mustering sufficient courage to ask a high school sweetheart for a dance.

"Factors" and "available blood-stopping mechanisms," that's what I saw and heard when luck ran out and skill was not enough. Placing a metal clip into a pool of blood was the available "blood-stopping mechanism" when there was a hole in the carotid big enough to insert a ballpoint pen. When the wrong artery was clipped or too much retraction occurred, it was a factor.

It was my education by proxy. I remained blameless while we conversed in ICU about what might have gone wrong. I stood by the side of my professors, protected by a vicarious immunity, as they told their patients' families that there was no hope. Eventually, mine would be the only white coat in sight as I crossed a waiting room to deliver a fatal report. As much as I might have wished, I knew I could never emulate Axel Olsen. He was the professor of neurosurgery at Hahnemann Hospital, just a short ambulance ride down Broad Street from Temple. He was renowned for his taciturn presence. He was tall and thin, and his hair was completely white. And unlike Dr. Scott, his expression seemed to be continually warding off intrusions. He almost never spoke and when he did it seemed painful, the effort too much. It was rumored that after one surgery he had approached the waiting family with his thumb down, and then was gone. Who was to say on the night Judith Halpern lay dying, that rather than relying on euphemism or asserting that I had marshaled all available resources, I might just as well have flashed a thumbs down, for all the good I had done?

CONSTRUCTION

What had Judith's family talked about for four hours after watching her being taken away? While she was driving, who knows where, how had they passed the time? Getting reacquainted can only take so long. "Remember me, Dad? I'm your daughter who hasn't visited in two years. The one who went to junior college and finally married. I'm supposed to be happy now."

"It's me, Dad, your son. Maybe you were right. I should have taken over the business."

Perhaps there had been very little to say, overwhelmed as they were by the thought of what Judith was going through. They may have been "small world" sociable, struck up conversations with the family members of other patients, all waiting in that common room. There would have been a hierarchy among them. The relatives of patients undergoing quadruple bypass, the name itself conjuring up a type of sweepstakes winner, would have been granted the most respect. Brain surgery for a tumor wouldn't have been far behind. A heart could be repaired, everyone knew that. It wasn't like the brain. Even without surgery, that was the organ that seemed to be failing in most of the transplanted parents who were now the object of attention.

If her family were readers, I didn't see them look up from their books as I approached. Lost in their own thoughts was more like it, as if Judith had visited them one by one, and then was on her way. That's where she might have gone after I excused her, after I had covered all but the nape of her neck and the shaved portion of her skull with those green drapes. She had been out in the waiting room as mother and wife beside the family that had been hers. Ben and the children were more than four hours older by the time she and I were done. Perhaps she counseled her son first, not advising what he should do with his life now, or insisting he spend more time with his children, but admonishing him to button his shirt. And she wasn't going to let him leave for school until he ate his breakfast. Of all the advice and loving she had ever given him, perhaps that was what had come back, until he could almost smell the fragrance in her hair as she leaned to kiss him good-bye, making sure not to catch the skin of his neck as she zippered his jacket closed. A different woman had visited the daughter, reminiscing about how they had closed the door to her room and then sat on the double beds, talking about periods and boys, men and training bras. As for Ben, he wouldn't have been sure who had come by — although someone had made certain his collar was turned down and that he hadn't spilled his coffee. Judith had been gone to him for some time, lost like everything else in the bright sun that rose in their ocean view bedroom window each morning. Even with air-conditioning, he had to close the drapes until that burning circle carried over the roof. He was napping as I approached. His daughter whispered in his ear and took his hand. The son stood. I could see Judith in his face, the same cheeks. I had stopped by the surgeon's dressing room and had picked out one of the white coats with the hospital's insignia to cover my scrubs. I wanted to represent more than just myself. I began with the routine, no hint of what I would have to tell them.

"The operation's over. It was a tumor, and although the permanent sections won't be available for three days, at least from initial reports it's a type that can't be completely removed."

Considering what I would eventually have to tell them, what better way to start? Brain cancer was in their minds now, without my having used the words or described what might be Judith's progressive deterioration. And a moment of respite occurred to me, as if Judith's destination offered some solace. I knew where she had driven. She had simply taken a short cut, waved good-bye from that improbable convertible and had taken off without us all. I continued on about her condition rather than the person who I knew was gone. I shared more details about "it," about the tumor.

"The growth seemed to extend to the area of the brain where breathing is controlled. It was quite vascular. She's on her way to the intensive care unit. I think the first thing we have to see is how she tolerated the surgery. We plan to keep her on the ventilator, to keep breathing for her tonight. But I am concerned."

They looked at me as if we all knew there was more. Her daughter, whether to support herself or her father gave me the opportunity to take them all back from the edge, away from the cemetery and the thought she'd never speak to her mother again.

"Can this be treated with cobalt?"

"Yes, if she recovers from the surgery and the quality of her life is such that she and you would wish to hold on to what she has, that's what we'll recommend."

Goddam me. Why couldn't I give them at least a little time? Hadn't they been out there for four hours? Hoping for what? That she would at least have a little more time? After all didn't the surgical plan include a simple biopsy if the tumor couldn't be entirely removed? All the daughter was asking for was a little more time. Couldn't I see that? "If she recovers" had struck a note.

I stopped then, told them that I wanted to check on her condition in the intensive care unit. That was fair. I didn't know for sure that she wasn't going to make it. I was always dispensing hope to patients and families with generosity; why not a little to myself every now and then? I knew this hope was hollow and insubstantial, as fleeting as the lost faces I had seen through the microscope. Now the son asked if she were breathing on her own and the machine just helping. I said that's what we would be waiting to see, but I was concerned that perhaps her breathing might not return.

If they seemed confused it was merciful. I could have elicited more questions, educated them about uncontrollable bleeding and brain swelling. But what would have been the purpose? That they were to be tested wasn't in doubt, but the material wasn't didactic. They were scheduled for one of life's practicals, the loss of a mother and wife. Let them consider what I had said, let the sounds of the words and phrases pass through and among them with the awful truth. When I added that it might be several days before we could be sure of her condition, it simply took Judith further away, beyond their collective voice and entreaty to return. The son and daughter knew. Ben was stunned, the way he had seemed in my office only days before. He looked down as if lost in some reverie, or as if he had found Judith who was beyond the rest of our recall. Was this my style, some half-effort at obscuration and refuge in the technical? I had been given euphemism and military precedent, but when it came to using both I had defaulted to delay.

Since Judith was not yet in the ICU and the effects of the anesthetic might still be suppressing her functions, I savored the possibility that she might recover. While I talked to her family I wondered to myself whether had I taken the biopsy from a different angle, focused on a different plane, perhaps removed more bone to begin with, I might have accomplished my purpose without hurting her.

I suggested that I return to the ICU and promised to give them an update on her condition. I left them in their stunned silence.

The nurses in the intensive care unit had attached their monitors and were going about their routine as if there were still a point to it. The respiratory therapist was adjusting the settings on the ventilator. Judith's internist was there. He just happened to be in the hospital. He listened to my euphemistic description of what had happened, the "inoperability" of her tumor. I didn't add what was occurring to me which was, if that were true, why the hell did I operate on her in the first place?

The first bedside examination extinguished whatever hope I had that she might recover. Her eyes were unseeing, her pupils pinpoint in size and nonreactive. My closed hand pressed against her chest seemed unfelt. She neither reached up to pull it away nor grimaced with displeasure. She was beyond pain. I disconnected her from the ventilator, separating it from the tube that had been left in her trachea. I held the palm of my hand to its opening, hoping to feel, if not see, the slightest breath. The second hand of my watch completed one orbit without a tangible sign of life. There was slight movement when I stroked the surface of her eyes, just enough to make the diagnosis of brain death premature. Her condition did not suggest she would recover. At best I saw her in a nursing home, comatose and on a ventilator. She wasn't going to awaken to hear the news that her tumor was the type that could not be completely removed, even if the surgery had been uneventful.

The anesthesiologist chimed in, "It's not us. We've reversed our agents." It seemed apparent to everyone at that bedside that the patient, a woman who had been whole going in, was never coming back. Perhaps it was just my imagination, but no one spoke to me. It wasn't like being in a dugout with teammates who didn't want to jinx a pitcher seven innings into a hitless game. It was more like the word was out on the street, "This guy's trafficking in some bad shit."

But this wasn't the street. It was the Miami Heart Institute, in its recently built addition with four-star patient rooms, and an ICU fitted with the most sophisticated monitors available. They called that building a pavilion, had financed its construction with the gift of just one donor. The hospital had other benefactors of almost equal wealth on their roster. In the administrative offices they were called "heavy hitters." They had retired to South Florida and were eager to give some of their money away, a tax write-off and something to be remembered by. They didn't know then that medicine would change. There wouldn't be enough private money to keep the institution going. Fifteen years later it would be owned by a corporation that thought about closing it down when it was merged with St. Francis, barely twenty blocks north on Alton Road. It didn't take an accountant in Minneapolis to know the profit was eroding, not enough young people with insurance in the community to keep it profitable.

That pavilion's benefactor and other donors who received crystal bowls at black-tie "Affairs of the Heart," would be as unknown to a future CEO as a boy riding his skateboard past the doctors' parking lot, the one with the fieldstone wall and lights at either end that I had walked to after briefing Judith's family one more time, agreeing we'd meet in the morning to reassess her condition.

It was ten o'clock and quiet outside the hospital that night as Judith lay in her post-op coma. Crime was somewhere else, in Miami across the causeways or down in South Beach with the Marielitos. At that hour the most activity in the residential neighborhood that bordered the hospital would be a resident with a poodle or an Orthodox Jew walking with his wife. No cars passed. No one was walking his dog. There were a few clouds highlighted by the moon, and a night breeze off the ocean only blocks away. There was the sound of palm fronds rubbing against each other and I could hear the sprinklers that covered the patch of grass along the wall and smell the plumeria that the full-time hospital gardener had planted at either end. I stepped over the wall, only two feet high, and then for some reason turned back to look at the hospital and at the lights coming from the windows of the ICU.

That view of where Judith lay dying has never left me. The perspective itself is part of an indelible image. I am below in the night solitude looking up at those windows, at the silhouettes of the nurses, and of Judith's family ushered to the bedside. They approach her with the impossible hope that she will squeeze their hands. They convince themselves that she has, although it is imagined and can not be confirmed. And I seem to be in two places at once, turning in that fatigued afterlook, and somehow still at Judith's bedside, remote stranger to myself, the causative agent for her terminal state, isolated by the rueful conclusion to the anticipated surgery of that day. Sometimes the lone figure, forever hesitating by that car to glance at the hospital and the light-filled windows above, assumes yet another identity. He is the narrator in Frost's "Acquainted with the Night," having heard an "interrupted cry" from another street and unsure of who it was for, himself or the lost patient.

It is a portrait in which the imperious artist has captured, in the truth of his revelation, a doctor drawn to his patient by a vision of light and loneliness. It is an image that haunts the promenade of a gallery, my pictures at an exhibition, acquired over years of practice and remembered loss. It has defied time and my attempts at resolution and yet it has changed. The years since that night have peopled that futile intensive care unit and the floors above with other patients and colleagues who have died before their time. They gather there in that canvassed hospital unchanged from when I knew them. A young mother who was on a general surgical floor at Boston City Hospital during my internship is there. She was alive on afternoon rounds, recovering from abdominal surgery, only to be in agonal and useless respirations two hours later, seized by a pulmonary embolus that saddled her lungs like the night-skied horse of the apocalypse. There is the open boat survivor of a triumphant surgical tour de force, who came that far, rescued from a strangulating spinal tumor, only to go into shock and die in cardiac arrest while being fitted for a brace two days after surgery. Next to him lies a stroke patient, whose aneurysm surgery was delayed for twenty-one days and then reacted to a drug-induced elevation of his blood pressure with a second and fatal hemorrhage. They are the casualties of fate and technology who shared the terribly fragile nature that is our existence.

None of the images fade. Instead the artist has continued to add to his work. "Judith's Pavilion" seems its inescapable title.

The hospital portrayed is not renown for research or miraculous cures, but simply because Judith and her fellow patients are never discharged. The nurses never go home. I have never driven away in my car to family and rest. And Judith's family never collect themselves, resolved to the unthinkable, but wait for their ten minutes every four hours, to beseech the unhearing.

PART TWO

Rounds

APPEASEMENT

It is to Judith's pavilion that I have admitted, confined, and confessed my failures, and not just my own, but all the patients who might otherwise haunt me, refuse to be buried or rationalized or forgotten. They are more than shadows seen through a window. They walk the halls or wave to me from their beds.

Margaret Clarke is there. She was the first patient on the neurosurgical service at Temple University Hospital with a halo brace. A metal ring encircled her head with four pins projecting through the scalp into the outer table of her skull. Four rods descended from that halo and were incorporated into a plaster vest that encased her upper torso. Only when she turned her body could her neck and head follow. The bones in her cervical spine were cancer-ridden and had outlived their usefulness. The rods and pins of the halo were supporting her head. To some that brace might have seemed an instrument of torture. To Margaret it had been a godsend. It had taken away most of her pain, the pain that never slept, the sentry to her every movement. Before the brace, it had seemed as if a beast would set upon her with the least of provocations — when she moved her head on the pillow, or tried to sit for her morning tea. The brace had kept the beast at bay. Sometimes she seemed to be caressing those rods as if combing locks of her hair. When she turned it appeared as if she were waving from a carriage, accentuating the impression of a royal bearing. Until her last admission to the hospital, I would see her walking the corridors of the neurosurgical floor, accompanied by her husband Henry, as if she were a Queen awaited at some formal tea. More than that brace with its four-posted canopy conferred upon her the mantle of royalty. The sharp lines of her face would have seemed regal even if her chin were not held continually erect. There was a kindness to her eyes as if she were acknowledging with shyness the loyalty of her subject. Her voice was thin and high-pitched although always soft in content. When she spoke it seemed a generous pronouncement. To see her husband's meaty hand grasp her delicately perching fingers evoked the image of a nursery rhyme, a rotund chef startled by a blackbird flying from his pie.

But it was clear that Margaret was not about to fly, or move in sudden startle. Still, there was a freedom to her movements. It was as if the mad dog that had seized her neck and wouldn't let go was now caged behind the four rods of that brace. Her freedom was to move as she wished, sit up in bed, or walk, all the simple acts of life that in the land of the well merit little notice.

Home from the hospital, and when the weather permitted, it was to her garden, her world illimitable, that Margaret returned. There her nightstand with its coral tissue box and her dialed radio seemed a thousand miles away. It was the tending of living things that drew her there, her attempt to overcome her barrenness, the childless core that had led her first to hope and then to despair. Ten years earlier, she and Henry had tried to adopt but were told by an agency that they were too late, already in their forties. She had contented herself then, or so it seemed, with her neighbors' children, celebrating their birthdays and conspiring with their costumed appearances at Halloween. Twice each year she visited her sister in Maryland and showered her nieces and nephews with the love she had wished for her own. But all that could be called her own was in that garden. That's where she had done her nurturing since the pioneering days in their Levitown home, when Henry's trailer lot was one of only a handful of businesses along a ten mile stretch of U.S.1. None of the identical houses that had grown up around them had a garden like hers. Henry could envision her there, imagine her taking her gloves off just outside the screen door, when he would call home in the spring and summer simply to hear her voice. Once, not long before the end, he watched her weeding in her brace as if from a box, marking rows, retying plants, and saving cuttings in a wicker basket as if they would be useful for a magic potion. At that moment he had a fatal premonition that was so distinct he was forced to rub his eyes to obliterate the image of a grave stone where her roses still grew.

Margaret had been told that her cancer was beyond cure. One of the doctors had said that occasionally patients like her could live for years. Remissions were known to occur. Between the radiation therapy and the safety of her vest, perhaps she might be one of the lucky ones. She had responded to those words with the calmness of her garden. The cycle of growing things had taken hold of her. She knew she was past her bloom, not yet cut down, perhaps still a perennial. Why not one more spring to blossom in the joy of the living? If that were not meant to be, she had faith that there was something beyond her garden. Her only pain then was in her heart, for Henry, who she knew would be alone without her. These were her thoughts in that haloed garden, when she breathed the summer afternoon, and believed the beast to be somewhere else.

In the end, the beast returned. It laughed in its grotesque mutation and pursued her with renewed malice. Barred from inflicting pain, it began to rub against her spinal cord as it would a tree, pawing at the ground, waiting to drag her away. It had chosen a structure as fragile as the most delicate stem in her garden, one she might have worried over in a heavy rain or silently asked a night breeze to be still in its turn. At last her body signaled it could stand the pressure no more. Margaret lost the sensation of temperature. She thought it strange when the washcloth that Henry held against her thigh didn't feel warm. He had always been meticulous about her care, knew about intimate things. When bathing her, he would caress her feet and legs with an unhurried rhythm. On this night, in the absence of that familiar warmth she decided to remain silent. But the next evening, when once again that nighttime wash was neither hot nor cold, she told him. Henry apologized and said something about thoughtlessness and distraction. But he understood it wasn't that. When he went to reheat the cloth he had kept his hands under the faucet until he couldn't stand the burning anymore, and then a bit longer. He had tried to appease the beast with his own pain. It would have none of it and instead just rubbed against the tree and pawed the ground some more with a sullen insistence. Henry returned to Margaret with his hands still red and steam on his face. She could see and smell the heat, but couldn't feel it. Then she knew too and saw all.

Still it was her nature to think of him.

"Thank you, that's much better," was what she had said.

Later, as she listened to his breathing from inside that halo, she found she couldn't feel her feet anymore, couldn't make the sheets stir with her legs. She awakened him.

"I think it's best we go to the hospital."

It was what she had dreamed of saying all those barren years, fully bloomed and ripened and knowing it was the time. If only she were having contractions now, counting the minutes between them, as her sister had. Her suitcase would be packed with a nightgown and robe and she would glance at her garden as her husband helped her into their car and delivered her to her joy. But she wasn't feeling contractions, or anything else for that matter. She told him then that she couldn't move her legs. He held her and whispered that he was sorry, that it would have been better if he had pressed her about the washcloth, had called the doctors then. He remembered their warning, "Call us if she complains of weakness, or has any loss of sensation." Both of them had kept the secret. The halo brace had saved her for a while, but they had grown tired of hiding from the beast. It was time for the cage to be unlocked.

I was the resident who admitted her to the hospital for the last time. The pin I used to test her sensation left drops of blood on the skin of her legs as if she had been tending roses. She reported that she felt no pain from the sharpened point until just below her neck. A shroud was being drawn upon her. The resources of the hospital were in place. If she were to agree, she would be taken to the operating room. We would search for the beast and cut it out, or try to undo what it had left behind. Instead, she apologized for having kept everyone awake, and took pains to assure me that her decision was not meant to be disrespectful. She said that she knew she was beyond help, that what we were offering wouldn't be enough. She seemed grateful when I accepted what she had said and was relieved that I hadn't tried to convince her otherwise. Then she slept. Perhaps she had a dream that the beast was sitting on her, making it difficult for her to catch her breath, then forcing a paw into her mouth. She awoke to see more doctors and understood that it wasn't a paw. An anesthesiologist had placed a tube in her throat. The top of her chest moved as she heard the sound of the respirator. While she had slept, the ability to breathe and move her arms had been lost.

The halo brace which had for a time relieved her pain assumed the confines of a prison then. For the next eight days she remained within those bars. The tubing of the ventilator extended to her as a last link. Paralyzed and unable to speak, she mounted with prisoner-like defiance her version of a hunger strike. She had enlisted Henry's support, her unwavering subject to the end. They communicated through her eyes, most superficially through a system of blinking her eyelids, one for yes and two for no. That was how she had made her first edict known. There would be no tracheostomy. The general surgeon who had been consulted to perform the procedure had explained how she would be able to speak and resume eating. When Henry leaned over the bed to ask if that was what she wished to happen, he saw the answer before she closed her eyes, twice, however briefly. It had been more to convince the surgeon of her will that she had performed that certain signal. There was to be no feeding tube either, no diet that bypassed taste and swallow that might extend her sentence indefinitely. Were it not for the intravenous fluids her pardon might have been granted within hours. Instead, eight days passed before she mercifully began to bleed, a last fatal bite that had lost its sting. By then she had withered inside that brace. We could have taken it off; the damage was done. Her pain had been relieved by a terminal lack of feeling and the beast was somewhere else. One last transformation remained. The rods of her halo brace became a trellis and Margaret climbed away from that place.

I had watched Margaret and her husband in that room, she in her determined parting and Henry in his last nurturing task. And he looked at her and would speak to me as if she had just presented him with an infant daughter.

ELEVATION

In Judith's pavilion there is an elevator that is always manned. On the night that Margaret dies, as the doors enclose Henry for the last time, I can almost hear him say, "Good evening, Hampton."

Hampton was the black elevator operator in the main building of the Philadelphia medical school where I spent the summer of 1963 after my sophomore year in college. My biology professor at Lafayette, Louis Stableford, had arranged for me to receive a research grant intended to place college students within a medical school setting. Each morning it was Hampton who ferried me to the eighth floor neurology suite.

"Eight, please."

"Yes, sir, Doctor." He had done it again, awarded me the title six years before my due. It was his ritual with every student in his charge. We were all doctors, from college through the actual four years of matriculation. He conferred those degrees with graduated calculation. He knew to what we aspired and carried us all along the way. He would nod a reassuring, "It'll be all right," to the stiff-collared admission candidates riding to the interview of their careers. He measured his pace more slowly when the last library students of the day decided to give it a rest. It was as if he were immersed in their studies through his own ponderous reflections. In the morning he was coffee, no cream or sugar, to the secretaries and the nurses. None of them would think of starting their day without a "Good morning, Mr. Hampton." He wore brown pants with suspenders and printed sport shirts. He never sat on duty. The wooden seat that the Otis Elevator Company had ingeniously built into the wall remained fixed in its upright position. His riders' attentions naturally focused on the back of his large round head. His closely shaved gray hair revealed the folds of his scalp. Since he would recite some homily of the day, a weather update, or what was to be performed that night at the outdoor concert at the Dell, there was the illusion that watching his scalp could substitute for seeing his hidden lips. It was an effort to prevent the message of the day from being lost between floors.

Hampton was in the perfect occupation, therapeutic in itself. What better way to handle an uncontrolled epileptic than to keep him in an elevator filled with doctors, some of them real, who would know how to protect his airway and prevent him from biting his tongue if he had a seizure? The worst that could happen when he had one of his occasional fits was that all of his passengers exited at the basement. Afterward he would be taken to the emergency room where he would sleep off any residual effects along with a contingent of frequent-flier drunks. I almost remember a bite block taped to his elevator wall, like a fire ax or extinguisher, everyone knowing, "IN CASE OF OPERATOR SEIZURE — ."

Perhaps it was one of those seizures that alerted the chief of neurosurgery, Paul Wagner, to Hampton's plight. Wagner had added seizure surgery to his repertoire and had offered to help the medical school's beloved elevator operator. As for the patient, of course he'd consent to the surgery. Didn't he carry Dr. Wagner to his office floor and down many times each day? "A fine gentleman," was Hampton's first reaction, "as are they all, always a 'Good morning, Hampton.'" If the operation were successful he might not even need the epilepsy medicine that caused his gums to thicken and seemed to make him sleepy. In some respects they were a natural team. Hampton's voice was melodious and full, thespian despite its cornered projection. Wagner's was somewhat high-pitched, just enough to strain the comfort of his listeners. They were to converse during the operation. Hampton was to be awake so that he might answer questions and perform simple tasks as the surface of his brain was electrically stimulated. The goal of the surgery was to identify and remove the portion of his brain responsible for his seizures.

I was granted permission to observe that surgery and arrived in the operating room just after the incision had been made. The local anesthetic had done its job. There seemed to be no pain. There was the sound of holes being drilled in Hampton's skull, like a tire being changed. Since the area of the brain suspected of causing the seizures was the temporal lobe cortex, it was necessary for Dr. Wagner to "elevate" the temporal bone. It is a part of the skull that cannot be removed simply by cutting bone between a series of holes. Its widened base must be broken, like bending a limb from a tree until it snaps. Access to Hampton's brain required his skull to be fractured.

Wagner cautioned his patient, "You may hear a little noise now." He didn't want Hampton to be startled by the sound of breaking bone. There was perhaps another reason for that thoughtful warning. Hampton had been endowed with a skull that was more than just thick in its vault-like proportions. If the security of the skull, its ability to remain impenetrable to errant missiles launched upon some prehistoric savanna, was an indication of an evolutionary advance, then Hampton was at the forefront. Pity that mankind's survival upon this planet seems so threatened. For the true appreciation of the protective benefits afforded by his head might take millions of years to appreciate. It would be ten more years before I would encounter a skull of such apparent advantage. As the chief neurosurgical resident, I had been called to the emergency room to see a patient who had walked in complaining of a headache. His blood pressure was noted to be elevated and he was about to be triaged to the medical clinic when a nurse noticed dried blood in his hair. She kept him in the department until he was examined by one of the doctors, who found what seemed to be two puncture wounds in the scalp. The skull Xray revealed that they were entrance wounds. My patient had been shot twice in the head. The bullets had just managed to penetrate his almost impenetrable skull. But they had been so wasted in that effort that there was neither the momentum nor apparent desire to go further. His brain had been spared. Later, it was discovered that he was a drug dealer. Had he never presented himself for treatment of those headaches, his wounds might have healed on their own and he might have never realized that his life had been threatened and only for a time saved by that advantaged skull.

But Hampton had not been skimming from the top, and his neurosurgeon was not a hit man dispatched to exact retribution upon an unsuspecting middleman. Wagner's imperfect voice above the drapes was intended to be reassuring. Hampton for his part must have had some sensation of the oxygen tubing placed around his neck with the two-pronged nasal inserts. The surgery hadn't been uncomfortable to that point, just about what they had told him it would be. He had been given some sedation as well. He might have been feeling a little high, close to dreaming about the ups and downs of his daily work. Not to say he was entirely removed. It would be necessary for him to report what he was feeling, to indicate if his right arm were tingling, and to count from one to ten when asked to do so.

Wagner might have already been looking ahead to the point where he would decide which few millimeters of cortex he could take and still have an elevator operator. The trick was to remove enough brain to extinguish the potential for seizures and still leave Hampton's version of "Yes sir, doctor," at full speed. It was in anticipation of Kubrick's *2001*. Wagner didn't want to hear a ponderous rendition of "Daisy, Daisy, give me your answer do." And he knew that the results of Hampton's surgery would become common knowledge among his colleagues and co-workers. If Hampton were to end up less coming out than going in, "Turned him into a vegetable," would be the medical school scuttle-butt. It could happen. Take a functional human being, an elevator operator, several seizures a month despite taking his anticonvulsants, and before someone could say, "son of a bitch," he might be in a nursing home, resident without dossier, remembered only by his family. His wife would sit by the bedside every day, bring her lunch in a paper bag, an orange and some crackers, and thank Jesus he was still alive. At the end of the day she would take her bag, with the uneaten portion of the orange, and sit on a bus for the hour's ride home, one transfer to West Philadelphia.

The warning was repeated, "You'll hear a little noise now." Then Wagner asked for a more substantial instrument than the one he had been using to force that temporal bone to its breaking point. The working ends of the periosteal elevator and dural separator were too delicate to get the job done. It had been like trying to pry open a manhole cover with pencils. The more force required, the greater Wagner's concern about one of those instruments slipping and unintentionally stabbing the brain.

"Did you ever see a skull this thick?" he asked no one in particular. It's likely that had he valued the opinion of anyone else in that room he wouldn't have become a neurosurgeon in the first place. It was time to improvise.

"Give me an osteotome." His request linked neurosurgery to orthopedics. It was what a neurosurgeon who was planning to lean over a patient with all his weight would require, reluctantly conceding, "I would have gone into ortho if I wanted to use a tool like this." The instrument had a polished and sharpened two-inch, crowbar-like end, making it easy to imagine on a wooden table, the one the jury would keep their eyes on throughout the entire case. The state would have introduced it into evidence as the weapon the defendant had used to brutally assault the victim. In its commonly assigned neurosurgical task, the subtle curvature of its working blade accomplished a bloodless stripping of muscles and ligaments from the spine. But it wasn't ordinarily requested in the course of a brain operation, unless before the scalp prep and draping, the head holder had been found jammed into the table. A stroke of improvisation would be needed then to pry the goddam thing loose. But under the circumstances, — "Jesus look at the size of that skull," — osteotome seemed like a perfect fit.

By that time, despite the repeated warnings, "You may hear a little noise," it seemed natural to forget that Hampton was awake. It wasn't the kind of detail to be remembered when surgery requiring brute force was to be done. But Hampton was hearing everything. It wasn't just euphemisms any more, "factors" and "situations," code words designed to blend into the sound of his breathing and the hiss of the oxygen catheter. What began as, "I'll take the ten Barde-Parker," instead of, "Hand me that scalpel," had become, "I'm gonna get that son of a bitch off if it kills me." Although it didn't seem at the time that Wagner was the one at greatest risk.

The osteotome slid underneath the opened part of Hampton's temporal bone perfectly. Wagner worked the resistance on the handle as if he were prying open an oyster. There was more than a pearl inside, there was the brain.

I continued to watch, college student on a summer research grant, admitted through doors marked Authorized Personnel to the inner sanctum. I had become aware of my own mask and OR greens and I heard the sound of my breathing with a rhythmic fascination. Standing somewhat away from the operative field, I could hear more than I could see. Still I wasn't prepared for what happened. I'm not quite sure anyone in that OR was, not the anesthesiologist, nor the patient, nor even Wagner, who had been steadily increasing the leverage on that inserted instrument. If anyone in that room could have had an expectation of cause and effect, a tactile premonition of audible result, it would have been the surgeon, as he tried to pry that "son of a bitch" up.

At last the base of Hampton's temporal bone gave way, and it sounded more like a gunshot than a breaking living thing. There seemed to be an echoing report. But there could be no doubt about the source. It was the sound of Hampton's skull fracturing, and not just any skull, but one that might have scoffed at a gun. It was as if that reluctant temporal bone had been the never-used retracted stool at Hampton's station. That's why he had never sat on duty. It was a premonition that had informed his ritual. To bend down that gold rimmed oak, must have struck him as obscene, and he wasn't prepared for it now. His cry that followed the sound of the shot seemed more involuntary reaction than disheartened complaint.

Then there was silence. No one spoke until Wagner quietly requested bone wax and gelfoam, agents needed to staunch the flow of blood from the fractured base of that imposing skull. Otherwise, silence, more pronounced for the memory of that shot and the cry that followed. It seemed that the sheer act of contemplation by those who had been present prolonged the event. Time was sound still traveling. That passage was soon overtaken by a noticeable change. It was reverie reversed. What had been heard reinterpreted as an assassin's act of awful destruction. Then, whether Wagner requested it by virtue of what he was seeing, or the anesthesiologist proceeded based upon his own observations, Hampton was put down. It was time for general anesthesia. There was no answer to one final, "Hampton, can you hear me?"

From that point on the surgery was just going through the motions. Hampton's cortex was exposed and revealed no apparent damage. Since he was anaesthetized, an approximation of the speech center was made, and Hampton gave up the portion of his brain suspected of causing his seizures. It was as if an insistence on completing what had been the purpose of the operation might be enough to make it turn out all right. There was quiet again. I thought I could hear the suture needles being placed back on the table, chorused by the flow of oxygen and the dispassionate marching tone of the heart monitor. There was no one talking on either side of the drapes. Far away the echo of that shot still reverberated. Maybe that's what it was like in a hospital in Sarajevo before they boarded up the windows in the operating rooms to foil the snipers.

Hampton never manned his elevator again during that summer. He wasn't back when I returned the next year. I heard that he was in a nursing home. It might have been the force of that concussive fracture from which he never recovered, as if the amplitude of the sound itself had shattered some fragile barrier within him. Or perhaps the subsequent harvesting of part of his brain had been overzealous. I don't know about his seizures, if they were less frequent or if he still needed medication. I think of him in that nursing home and in Judith's pavilion as shell-shocked more than anything else. He had become like the World War II veteran in the town where I was raised. Gaunt and always simply dressed, that familiar apparition walked with his head down, as if he were on his way from Bataan. Predating the long-distance runners with their designer body suits and Walkman headsets, he always seemed to be on the side of a road, no matter the weather or the time. His face was as expressionless as the trees of the season. He walked as if the traffic around him made no sound. It seemed as if his ears were filled with something else, like Hampton I suppose — relentless bombardment or a single shot made little difference.

MURDER

Perhaps I am distinguished from Hampton only by virtue of what fills my head, shell-shocked of a different sort, *Flitter, Flitter,* reverberating from the halls of Judith's pavilion. If there is respite, it is in the sanctuary of rooms in which friends reside. Bonds built on illness and profession, otherwise tenuous, are preserved there. I am summoned to the images of my lost affection, by the familiar and the unpredictable. Just as I check on Hampton, each time I perform a temporal craniotomy, consult with him as I apply my leveraged purpose, so it is to Ivan Uskov's room that I am called when a news report of some heinous crime becomes the public focus.

Ivan had prosecuted murder cases as an assistant district attorney in Philadelphia. He had been recruited to that office, persuaded to give up his lucrative practice as a defense attorney. It was Ivan, wooed from the side where money talked, who had the last say for the state. Depending upon which side of the courtroom one were sitting, Ivan could be Rasputin or his namesake, the Terrible. To see him was to picture him on the steps of a Russian Orthodox Church. His black hair, full mustache and pointed beard were icon-like, inspiring the suspicion that he had sprung to life from some gilded beam. His voice was priestly. He pronounced his words as liturgy, expunging any doubt about his purpose. How that wrath had ever served the guilty was his abiding mystery. His six-foot frame gave an impression of only the vertical, the lines of his face, the sharpness of his nose, even the unruly sprouting of his eyebrows, all upward, as if in anticipation.

We met in the last year of his life and at the end of my neurosurgical training. We were both in transition. I was a resident during his first admission to the hospital but was his attending physician when he died. I applied the first electrodes on the skin of his back in an effort to disguise his pain in a sense of vibration, and I performed the last of his three operations, a cordotomy, that almost unthinkable assault with a scalpel upon his spinal cord. All the while I came to know the man beyond his spreading cancer and the trial of his pain. It might have been the legal profession that he shared with my father which first drew me to him. Ivan knew the secrets of the trade, and the judges, and what it was like to address the jury in a high-ceilinged, dark-paneled courtroom, with the portrait vigilance of Jefferson and Lincoln upon him. And since I had not yet found my father in me, I looked to Ivan in that ongoing search.

As for Ivan, perhaps he found surcease from pain in my listening. There was therapy in his narrative. He told me about the part of his life he wished to share. Revisiting his history reversed our roles. I became the investigator, he the healer. I listened to the particulars of his life. He recounted details about his failed marriage, went on to describe his heaven-on-earth true mate, with whom he lived when we met, and who would nurse him until his death as if she were the wife of twenty-five years. She cared for him as mate and mother. She knew just the right combination of pillows to keep his pain at bay and it was she who tended to his digestive system at both ends of the food chain.

I met her in his room as she visited. Her name was Katherine. My shyness at the disparity of their ages and the similarity of ours made me concentrate on her dress more than her person. She wore tan leather boots and a gaucho skirt and a scarf that was slightly more than casual. She was Agnes Irwin privileged, straight to Vassar from that Philadelphia mainline preparatory school. Her features, which I eventually confronted, seemed to attend the Moore College of Art, charcoal sharp and portfolio confident, no need of makeup there. When she spoke, it was with a smile, her Ardmore diction flowing with the wisps of her thin blond hair. The irony was that it seemed as if she had awakened his long-dormant prostate, instigating a cellular revolution of the worst kind. It was a deadly palace revolt against ecstasies that had been all but forgotten during the waning years of his marriage. Those cells would hear nothing of the pleasures that had come to Ivan in his fifties. They refused their duty when pressed with increased demands, destroyed their fellow cells and then set out to take over the rest of the body, first the prostate, then the skeletal system and lungs. All we doctors could do was treat the pain. There was no chance for us to destroy this new regime. Its destruction would require a final Pyrrhic victory that only Ivan could achieve. I wonder if it was the last verdict he had heard, carried upon the breeze of his agonal respirations, after a year of torture, his moment of insight revealed, "The bastards are to be taken with you." The host of cells that were ending his life, that had inflicted pain upon him, reduced him to an infant in diapers with feces in the bed, the windows opened despite the cold;

they were going too. It was almost enough to inspire a change of will: "Get me to a crematorium."

He might have done just that, had it not been for his Russian Orthodox church and the elaborate, hours-long celebratory mass that awaited him. Rising smoke and Gregorian chants were to shepherd him to the other side. Russian mythology merged with Christianity in that church with its high windows and bearded clergy. The mourners were opposite-aisled, as if at a wedding. Instead of friends of the groom to the left and of the bride to the right, the choice was either respect and last love to Ivan, or social deference to his surviving widow. Ivan's casket was open. His waxed and rouged features were serene. It was a formaldehyde eradication of the cancer. Not quite as satisfying as the embrace of immolation, but savored to the last drop of that final cure. But his graven image at the foot of the altar in that Byzantine church had not yet rested its case. I resurrected him there, even before his admission to Judith's pavilion. He stood before the altar arguing that the only possible verdict that could be returned was murder in the first degree.

I had remembered a trial he had told me about as we sought his comfort. The defendant was a bow hunter who had slain his wife while she slept. In the mistaken impression that he was more cunning than his stalkers as well as his prey, he had smeared his dying wife's blood on the walls of their home. It was a Manson-like publication, punctuated with excrement, intended to prove beyond a reasonable doubt that only an insane man would slay his wife with arrows and then write his confession on the flowered walls of the parlor. In the midst of that Greek mythological funeral as I watched from the side of the lover, the wife slayer was to be tried again.

Ivan had pursued the hunter in relentless inquiry. It was what had made him a successful defense attorney. He hadn't survived three-hour funerals in that church for those who had crossed over before him, without refining his sense of contemplation. It rose with the smoke and the chanting to those high windows. It was his perspective when assigned to an unspeakable case. His investigation was illuminated by the same light that now settled upon the mourners who had chosen to honor him.

He examined the file as he might his own hands in meditation, or the collar line of a parishoner in the pew directly in front of him. The police report read like the lyrics in a hymnal. Ivan's hosanna was to beseech both judge and jury to reject the plea of the would-be insane. He had driven to the West Philadelphia row house where murder had left its stain. The bow hunter who had killed his wife had come upon her as she slept. She had tried to flee at the intrusion of a first wound, had run to the stairs, and then sat down when pierced by a second fatal arrow. Her husband was not done, but unleashed a third that transfixed her neck to a rung of the banister. She remained pinned there, a specimen of his errant skill. It looked to the police who gathered in the foyer below as if she had simply been waiting for them. She had sat on steps like those in her parents home as a child on a New Year's Eve, listening to the music and the sounds of glasses and laughter until it was midnight and her uncle had seen her and carried her down the stairs to the celebration. There had been no blood or cryptic message of confession on the wallpaper that night. Now, after the medical examiner ordered the sculptured rung and arrow to be transported with her, she was carried down again. They covered her with a blanket, all but her face, the arrow, and the wooden target too. The police photographer was so taken by the incongruous image cast against the parlor wall, that he sought to capture that moment on film. It was his one attempt at art which he simply buried in the file. But when Ivan saw that bloodied silhouette, it hardened his resolve for justice.

Ivan climbed those stairs and later ran his hand across the scrubbed walls that were meant to testify for the defense. He followed a trail back to police headquarters where he asked to view the contents of the cardboard box in which the evidence was stored. It struck him that there was something more than sportsman-like about those arrows. He wondered if arrows were like guns, had their own hierarchy from target to killing. Ivan had already proved he wasn't the kind of attorney who was reluctant to leave his office. And so he signed for one of the arrows, logged his intention for it to be taken off-site, to an archery store.

"Oh I remember now," the desk cop contributed. "The nut case who killed his wife with a bow and arrow. Must have thought she was a deer."

"Bad speller," added the cop.

But Ivan, who had discovered mysteries within mysteries during those funeral masses, found neither murder nor alleged insanity amusing.

"What would I use an arrow like this for?" he asked the man behind the counter, laying the evidence on glass beneath which knives lay, unsheathed and ripe for gutting.

The salesman was a hunter himself, thought the high point of each year was archery season for buck. Started building his tree stand in June. He still had some venison from last year's harvest in the freezer.

"Not for deer. See the tip? It's a broad-head six. Count 'em. That many blades will screw up your flight. Good for killing but you need to be right up to your prey. Work on hibernating bear, but that's illegal. I've seen 'em in magazines. We don't carry them here, there's no need to."

There wasn't a season for man.

Ivan, a defense attorney turned prosecutor, had his case. He asked the county detectives to find the source of those arrows and they did. The bow hunter, who had planned his defense, had left an unintended sign. It was his signature on a credit card receipt. He had charged those arrows along with his resolve two weeks before the death of his wife. All living things had been out of season then. He turned down murder three, twenty years. He was unable to convince the jury through his sobbing, that all he could remember was a nightmare. They knew about nightmares, had been given one of their own. It was Ivan holding that strange cross bathed in courtroom sunlight, an arrow in the rung of a banister. The verdict was guilty as charged, the sentence was life without parole.

The bow hunter who slew his wife still lives. He's found religion and is described as a model prisoner. He has an appeal pending, filed it himself. It asserts that there was tampering with the evidence. As for the state, Ivan rested his case. He was beyond the arrows of his loveless wife, murder, too, of a different sort.

"I'll ruin you socially and financially," was what she was alleged to have said. She made good on the latter, but by then it was of no real concern. The happiest period of his life, he once told me, was the time he spent with Katherine.

I remember my friendship with Ivan like a tragic opera that unfolded in three acts. His illness and funeral were the first and last, and between them was Katherine's unforgettable aria. On the day of his death, after it fell upon me to pronounce Ivan expired, Katherine and I left the hospital together. It was cold and raining as it should have been. We found shelter in a restaurant and settled into a paneled booth. While Ivan was being wheeled to the morgue, Katherine shared with me their brief history as she had lived it. She told me about how they had met at a church retreat and fallen in love spiritually and physically. I heard about the best of times, his gourmet cooking and the traveling they had done collecting icons. Had Ivan been searching for his father, too? She described the details of how she had cared for him over the last year, and except for his suffering, how she wished it might never have ended. She told me that when his pain had made him cry out, she couldn't move for it, felt that pain in her own body and then sobbed in the other room so that he wouldn't hear. Once she talked about the future as if he were still alive, and it was just a matter of time until he was discharged again and they could both go home. We both lost time in that confessional on the afternoon of his dying.

I just listened, his life and their story were hers for the telling. I no longer had healing to dispense, and as for absolution, none was needed. She seemed as beautiful in her grief as she had been in her nurturing. I saw her then as if in a portrait, her enigmatic smile meant solely for the object of her lost affection. What might have stirred in my resident's heart was laid to rest. Opera turned to requiem. Katherine had been to those funerals too. She knew that this was the eulogy she would never be asked to deliver.

Three days later Ivan's convicted widow had been restored as next of kin. I saw her for the first time then, tearless in the relative dark, surrounded by judges and lawyers. But Katherine held my gaze in that high church, bathed in the sunlight that burned away the whispers and glances and secret smugness of the wives who thought they knew her, a home wrecker. What home? And rising with the music and the rhythmic smoke was the peace she had bestowed upon my lost friend.

AFFECTION

I never saw Katherine again. I chose not to hear her voice or see that faint smile and suffer the guilt of a survivor. My memory of her was buried with Ivan. In his room in Judith's pavilion, after our discussion of some grisly crime, it is he who informs me of Katherine. Would that I had similar access to word about Anne.

Anne was college student to my residency, prospective bride and mate, not from history but by association. She was the patient whose life I wished to share outside the hospital. When she spoke of her brother at Princeton and the summer vacations she had spent on Martha's Vineyard with her family, I could imagine myself accepting a second cocktail from her father before dinner. He was a family practitioner, doctor to a rural community. His patients would have called upon him day and night for deliveries and dying. I could see her mother tending the rhododendron bushes that would have surrounded their home with the acceptance of a woman who had listened to her husband answer the phone and then quietly leave their bed for someone with a greater need. Why not such a life for Anne and myself? Early in her hospitalization for treatment of her myeloma, we had uncovered the common threads of our backgrounds. We were pre-megalopolis, suburban New Yorkers, Anne from New Jersey and I from Pennsylvania. We shared the best of both states, an accessibility to the Lincoln Tunnel by noon with the rest of the day for Manhattan. It didn't matter that we had been raised on different sides of the Delaware, our sign language was the same. I displayed a professional track, on my way to the American dream before it had ever been cast in doubt. Anne was studying for enlightened domesticity, before home economics and feminism had discarded that role. And if the absorption of topography had made me feel there was no place like home, then first loves had similarly imprinted my heart. Anne could have been Sheila, Mimi, or Karen. She succeeded those girls turning women who had informed my adolescence. I don't know who I may have been for her, but I tried to make him endearing. Just as my shyness and the fear of something more averted my eyes from Katherine, my unashamed gaze upon Anne spoke of an almost palpable freedom. Yet I was one of her doctors, if only the resident assigned to her care. We had not met in a library or found ourselves joined together at the wedding of mutual friends. Plato had to be the chaperon of our friendship.

At first Anne's illness had not seemed to cloud the future like some other cancer. Even the name was softer, more forgiving, "myeloma." Unquestionably it was her tumor of the blood, but it was treatable. I never understood exactly why she was on the neurosurgical service. It was something of a courtesy arrangement, friends of a friend who knew my attending. It seemed quite natural, for when Bill Buchheit wasn't being announced by Henning as the elevator doors opened, he was being paged for some outside call. And whether it was for a ski trip to Colorado, or horseback riding in California, it made no difference. He rode the social circuit of a bachelor neurosurgeon with the ease of a fictional character. But there was nothing make-believe about his surgery. If a patient had a brain tumor it was Buchheit who had better take it out. He was six feet tall, with the build of a linebacker and even the bald spot on the crown of his head seemed fitting. He combed his hair in licks, part way between school yard and dictator. It accentuated his duality. His name and face implied that in a not too distant village one of his relatives might have hidden from the Cossacks. But in his temporal form Buchheit could have been mistaken for an equal opportunity bigot. It was not malice, only a propensity for gossip that fired his pseudo-prejudice. He had first sat upon his high horse in the sunset of Eisenhower's America, when everyone knew their place. And it was Buchheit's resident. Why shouldn't I have chatted with Anne about our respective pedigrees? I had learned more than surgery from the man.

Her room was my refuge at the end of the day. After I had justified my presence by testing her strength and reflexes, my visit would turn social. As she spoke about whatever we had settled upon as my reason for lingering, I tried to remember where I had seen eyes like hers before. They were green, with lashes that seemed more delicate than the light. Her hair was straight and brown and casually settled upon her shoulders. Her face invited touching, blind love in a literal sense, its contours meant for Braille. What stories I read there, Helen of Troy and Joan of Arc and all the fires between. But the pause above her cheeks, the tentative rims of the hollow of her illness, made all the endings sad. To look at her was to submit without regret to a desire to tell her all, from first to last, secrets, weaknesses and dreams. There was no choice. It was the perogative of that face, the paradox of beauty, to wield so much power with so little effort and no definite promise of reward. Had we never spoken, I would have remained enamored of her. But the softness of her voice, the sympathy in her questions, and the focus of her attention made her face all the more unforgettable. She kept her robes buttoned at the neck — just as well. Her arms below the half sleeves were frail, but the translucent down was as much mystery as I could handle. It always seemed as if her hospital identity bracelet were about to slide from her wrist. I wish that it had, or that she had removed it at home, anticipating returning to college, restored to her family and authentic love.

After a month-long stay in the hospital, her condition improved and she was scheduled for discharge on a Monday morning. After I had spent that weekend off in the routine of youth's never-ending tomorrows, Anne just happened to have died on Sunday night. It was all wrong. Her tumor had been in remission.

I was driven by a need to find some answer, as if a clinical solution might wash away my grief. I followed her to the morgue. It was in the basement of the hospital where almost six years before I had stood with a contingent of my medical school class around the prosector's table with its organ scales and fluids draining into the big muddy. Didn't we all laugh when the pathologist had found a coin in the stomach of the corpse and Rocco had said, "I thought you couldn't take it with you." But this day, I knew I had made a terrible mistake. It was not the way I wanted to remember her. Her scalp had been turned down over that face. They had removed the top of her skull — not the side windowed flap of my surgical specialty — more like the crown of a Russian doll, dolls within a doll. Only there wasn't a new Anne inside. Instead her brain had been removed and placed in a heavy jar. Her optic nerves had been severed without a thought of blindness, and all the springs and colors, sheet music and printed words in the world were as irrelevant to those stumps as the overhead fluorescent lights that cast her jaundiced skin in its raceless hue. They had defused her, cut the carotid arteries and the cranial nerves that had tethered her to life. Her body seemed more frail than I had realized, as if she had been in a camp. Her pelvic bones and pubis formed a sexless, irrelevant image that assaulted further my mistaken journey. I should have remembered her fully clothed in the nightgowns and robes she wore, with flowers at her bedside. Remembered her as she sat in her bed and spoke of the things that were common to us. That was who I wanted to remember, not an eviscerated carcass on a shining aluminum table, more disease process than lost friend, the spots in her liver and lungs pointed out like constellations in an indifferent universe. Had I given voice to my heart I would have said, "For Christ's sake give her up. Why the hell are we doing this anyway?" But I was presumably a doctor in training, expected to take it all in, without considering who she had once been.

What had I hoped to accomplish there anyway? To see Anne one last time? To understand what had happened to her so that I might imagine our being together at the end? Did I wish to attend that terminal loneliness? If her death had been caused by a blood clot, dislodged to her lungs from a vein in her leg, there was nothing I could have done. She might have been saying good-bye to her mother on the phone or pushing aside her tray before getting out of bed. There would have been a quizzical look on her face that turned to something beyond terror when she tried to take a breath and it made no difference. Perhaps I would have held her then as if we had taken refuge in a closet from a firestorm only to discover there was no air.

No one had been in her room when she died. It was the aide who collected the meal trays who found her on the floor. She thought it was just a robe at first. She went running for a nurse who called a code, had the operator announce the euphemism for a patient whose heart had stopped. The interns and residents who were in the hospital converged on her room. Some could barely fit inside because of the crowd. They cleared the doorway and brought in the defibrillator. The only rhythm on the monitor was from the compressions of her chest. They all watched as if it were the world series, or Kennedy's funeral cortege. It was obvious that she had been dead for some time. How the hell often did those nurses check on her? Then there was nothing left but the paperwork. "Anybody know her?" I wasn't there, just the chart to tell them she had been scheduled for discharge in the morning. There was a note indicating that a decision had been made not to transfuse her. She was young enough to replenish her low blood count on her own. They took her away and put her in a freezer until the next morning, when the autopsy could be done.

It wasn't so much what I had found in that morgue as what I lost. Had I been asked for identification before being allowed to leave, I'm not sure what papers I might have shown. Perhaps just answered with a shrug, if asked what had been my purpose there. I went in as a college student who had made it through medical school, interned at Boston City Hospital, and then with an unbroken stride had begun his neurosurgical training. But I had been an impostor, masquerading as a doctor, without giving up the boy who had wanted to be a neurosurgeon since seventh grade. What had I expected? That I would be allowed to dress up in a white coat, attend meetings, actually do some surgery, and then not pay a price? I had walked into that morgue presumably as an investigator and a scientist, thinking

I could purge my grief through the salvation of knowledge, and I had been transformed into a ghost who had seen himself. I had been with Anne in the end after all, not lying beside her in the forbidden fulfillment of a natural affection, but embraced by our common mortality. I grieved for us both, carcasses on an aluminum table, deorganed and deafferented, and for what?

Still the paperwork was not done. Almost a year later I received a note from Anne's mother. The stationery was engraved with the script, *A Note from Anne.* She wanted to thank me for my care. What struck me, beyond the extended interval between Anne's death and the expression of her mother's gratitude, was that stationery, *A Note from Anne.* I visualized her room and the desk that had held that box of notes untouched for almost a year. I saw her mother there. She had decided to recreate her daughter's habits, to write a note. It was yet another effort to appease her grief which had not abated with a turning of the seasons. Perhaps the pen did feel somewhat different in her hand, her posture, more erect. But to whom to write? Why not to the resident she had met during Anne's last hospitalization? He seemed to have had the time for a visit every day, not just in and out with false promises. It seemed to her that he had acted like a suitor. She thought that he would understand. He had suffered too.

As I held *A Note from Anne,* there was an interval of time between the reading and my comprehension. It wasn't a second or a year, just light on a paper in my hand and a casual turning. Just long enough to question, who was the author? Was it Anne, magically back in her room, in her embroidered robe, with flowers on the night stand and a finely laced comforter upon the bed? The uncertainty in that interval was our state of grace, and then it was gone. I didn't realize at that moment what her mother had done for me, how she had given me one last moment with Anne. I wrote back to her, something about "the note from Anne" and about "unspoken dreams." I suppose it was enough to confirm her suspicions.

Some days, from the hallway outside her room I see Anne in Judith's pavilion. I take care not to signal for her attention but content myself by simply watching. I have learned not to enter, for there is only one way out. It is past an aluminum table with a drain at its base from which I avert my eyes. And I do not stop and try to understand the muffled voice that speaks to me through a turned-down scalp.

PART THREE

The Morgue

DISSECTION

A glass jar draws my attention next. Its occupant is suspended, floating on a nearly transparent net, bathed in formaldehyde. Thick glass and a heavy grooved lid seals its charge. The jar was designed for that. A specialty works in West Philadelphia had been approached by one of the first neuropathologists. "I need a container approximately twelve inches in diameter and equally high. Something sturdy, but glass, so that I can see the contents." It seemed he was concerned about conspiracies, or perhaps he thought that something might be looking out.

"We'll use it for a brain, until the anatomic relationships are fixed. Keep it from disintegrating into a paste-like amorphous mass."

He aimed to study structure, unlock the secrets of function and the clues to our demise. The glassmaker understood exactly. He made the prototypes from which others were subsequently copied and mass-produced. Made them so that there was a sense of inviolability to those jars as I first saw them, sitting in rows on a wooden worktable in the closet-like room devoted to brain cutting in the Department of Neurology. It was during another summer of research and observation at the Philadelphia medical school, where I had watched Hampton's surgery. I passed that room and those jars many times each day. They seemed immune from errant mishap, safe from any dislodged instrument that might fall from an overhead shelf. The arrival of a new addition was announced by an incongruous clanking of glass against glass. It would set the other inhabitants to rocking gently like sloops at anchor in the wake of a passing launch. If one of the neurology residents chose to rearrange those jars, it seemed a game, some sleight of hand to challenge my powers of observation. Which the genius? Which the idiot? Could I pick out the one who was patiented for thirty years at Philadelphia General, not far from where those jars were made, the man with hands for a face, who never spoke and was unable to control his bowels, who had spent his days and nights in a corner of his ward, rocking with his eyes closed like some clock that never needed winding? A succession of orderlies had cleansed and fed him.

The heavy lids on those jars prevented the odor of formaldehyde from marking us like workers in a stockyard. It was a stigma that could turn a cosmopolitan subway rider, called professor at work, to a pariah in transit. Fellow passengers would move away or turn their backs, amid the noise and dust of the underground passages and the open wastebaskets that rushed by at each station. There was a warning to that smell, as if olfaction were imprinted with some lost memory of the race. Its message was about having passed too far, ending up at a last stop from which there could be no return. It didn't wash off, despite the soap or fragrance used, but set about denaturing the skin of the careless or the distracted. I assumed that's what Dr. Mills, the resident who had invited me to observe his brain-cutting session, meant by his warning: "The less precise you are, the more you become like the specimen."

Mills was a psychiatry resident completing his neuropathology studies. For me, his psychiatric background added to his mystique. One day he would enter the thoughts of the living, turn their misperceptions and phobias around, and cut through their neuroses like a scalpel through tumor. And Mills was British. It was as if he had personally known the authors who had first described in the *Proceedings of the Royal Academy* the maladies which now bore their names. His bearing was erect. It made him seem as if he were looking down at the rest of us, not from some conceit, but by a natural station conferred from birth. From his slightly raised eyebrows, his sharp nose, and his thin lips, there arose an air of skepticism. It was better that his patients were to be looking at the ceiling as they revealed all. His smooth forehead and sparse, carefully combed hair completed the sense that nothing was amiss in his structured world. He was a man who lived his philosophy. He was committed to not becoming like the specimen. He had whispered that admonition, as if there was something more than just advice at hand. I saw it in the way he donned a plastic apron and latex gloves and bade me do the same before we could proceed. He laid out his instruments as if setting a place at a table. There were two wooden-handled knives, more like spatulas. The rounded edges of the blades seemed designed for slicing butter. Next to the knives were two silver forceps. The larger had right-angled working tips for the dissection of blood vessels within the recessed contours of the brain. There was a scalpel with a newly inserted disposable blade, number ten. He would use it to incise the tenacious bands of arachnoid, the filamentous binding that enveloped the brain. A magnifying glass revealed the rough wooden surface of the work counter. Small specimen containers were arranged alongside a wax pencil. Mills was prepared to harvest what might catch his attention and continue his search for the truth under a microscope, progressing from cosmos to cell.

On the previous day he had selected the brain he planned to study. He had removed the lid and placed the heavy jar with its occupant under a faucet on one side of the double sink at the far end of the table, adjusting the tap to maintain a constant overflow, an exchange of water for formaldehyde. The gentle stream offered a mantra to his purpose. It became part of the lab's ambiance, as if some ritual of purification were in progress. The brain rested on the frail netting like an unearthly catch. Deprived of familiar vault and active body, it seemed filled with regret for all the lost world. In my reverie inspired by the sound of the flowing water, it seemed that until the actual dissection had begun, there was something whole to the part, a semblant being floating in that jar, suspended in time as well as place. I wondered if somehow it had heard the running waters of life and time, and listened again to what had passed from its mother's womb to that lab and all that came between. It had emerged from the sea in a primitive cellular shape and inexorably passed from consciousness to this uneasy sleep. Now it was past holding on and beyond drowning.

If that brain had heard the sound of the water, then why not imagine it straining to see through the darkness as well? I thought I saw some slight movement in the jar. Then I forced myself to return to the clinical present, and whoever it had been was swept away.

Mills was ready to begin. We were gowned and gloved and wore glasses. Did he think the thing might spit? It seemed he had assigned a malevolent presence to that brain, and in his warning not to become like the specimen had cast the moment as us against it. "It" was not simply a brain that had lain in wait for weeks and had watched the comings and goings in the lab. "It" was that other world, the one of specimens, living and dead. In his future specialty the specimens at their worst would merely speak of torment and delusions. Now there was something tangible, a structure he would need to touch. Since he was neither rocking in a corner, nor bathed in some endless cleansing stream, he had set his priority in simple terms, "not becoming like the specimen."

He began the dissection, showing me the way to the nature of being. There was a sense of being drawn into the object of our study. A major artery on the undersurface of that brain seemed to exert with its branching tributaries a tenacious hold on what had been the living, drawing us into another world. Mills removed that vessel and others of similar size as if stripping vines from an aging wall. Then he set upon that brain as if it were a loaf of bread. It reminded me of the e. e. cummings poem, "Here is little Effie's head/whose brains are made of gingerbread." There were no crumbs. When he put down the first knife the brain was left in slices, from front to back, from the repository of emotion and memory to the last segment of the brain stem. I was struck by the diminutive size of that last slice that fell on its side like a coin. It had remained hidden throughout evolution at the point where the spine articulates with the skull. It had been secure there in its seemingly inconsequential station. As other functions passed by with words and images, conceits and avarice, they must have acknowledged the appropriateness of such a location for the untiring controller of respirations.

Mills began to rearrange the slices, as if each were a card. There were new hands to be dealt, not so much to be wagered as studied. But Mills was more interested in the past. He dealt three consecutive hands as if one for himself, one for me, and one for a guest of honor. He studied each surface with a magnifying glass. He pointed to areas of involution or staining as if they might still be alive, and described in his British formality the significance of his findings. He became engaged by a small benign tumor that he found in a hidden crevice. It may have been the only one he ever excised with a scalpel. He harvested small square sections and deposited each with fine forceps into a waiting glass container. He filled the tissue requirements of the pathologists, and the assorted research projects. He labeled each section in its own container with names like basal ganglion, parietal cortex and cerebellum. The titles seemed to cast their own spell and called me to that time when his mastery might be mine. All the while his labor was remarkable for his announced intention, "to keep from becoming like the specimen." He wiped the instruments frequently on a clean white towel. An odd bit of matter was unacceptable. He would stop whatever he was doing until its proper disposal. He frowned with the effort as if worried that a speck might have gotten away.

By then it was too late to put the pieces back together. Even if he had tried, their orientation was lost. The session was over. He placed what was left of what had once been a brain in a brown plastic bag. He poured formaldehyde into the small containers and quickly covered each floating section with a black lid. The empty heavy jar and its ponderous lid were placed side by side to dry on a white towel. He washed the instruments with a mixture of enthusiasm and relief. The running water seemed to carry him from his fears. He washed the workbench down with equal flourish. His intensity set the remaining specimens gently rocking at their anchorage. With that I lost my detachment again. It seemed to me they were communicating among themselves like death row inmates who had watched the lights dim. If the brain we had dissected had given up all the moments of life that it had known, had they seen that, too? To what had those silent sentinels borne witness? Then, as if by a magnetic force, or some other trophic pull, those graying cronies faced the same way. I didn't know if they were turning away from us or perhaps toward something else.

The summer passed, and I have no recollection of seeing Dr. Mills again. But my time with him had become a defining event, described by his advice, "Don't become like the specimen." I thought of him as a soothsayer who had appeared at the edge of a forest. His words stayed with me as I finished college. In my biology labs they set my habits. Not becoming like the specimens was as important as identifying appendages or counting the segments of arthropods. "Don't become like the specimen" seemed equally good advice in the first year of medical school. Although there was no hope of avoiding the pale of formaldehyde that surrounded us the entire first semester, I nonetheless remained cautious in the presence of our embalmed cadaver. As it was progressively dissected, cannibalized into shreds of insertions and origins, I grew increasingly aware of the remnants of the day's lesson.

My surgical training refined further what Mills had said, made his advice as current as my next case. It occurred to me that as he had set out those instruments with calculated precision he was acting as defender of a faith. An infidel would be one who lost respect for what he did. To take a knife to the brain, either in its natural or post mortem state, required uncompromised diligence. His words had become less admonition than credo.

Almost a decade later I crossed paths with a fellow physician who had been in training at the medical school where I had spent my college summers. He was one of those individuals who merited respect as a quasi historian. His lines of communication to his alma mater had never been cut. He knew the personalities I could not forget, and what had happened to them. Elizabeth, the department nurse who had befriended me, had suffered a brain hemorrhage and was rumored to be in a persistent vegetative state. Dr. Kramer, the department chairman, had died. Richard Conrad, the resident with whom I had worked in the forgotten laboratory that held the memorabilia of the pioneers of Philadelphia Neurology and Neurosurgery, was practicing in New Hampshire. His three sons had dispersed to their own lives. Of the other residents, not much news. Almost as an afterthought his report concluded, "Remember the psychiatry resident who was rotating through? I think he was British, a Dr. Mills? I heard he committed suicide."

Suicide, my fabled doctor. How could that have happened? Had Mills, despite the conviction of his philosophy, become careless? It was not enough to place his death simply in the context of another psychiatric jumper. I suspected almost all of them fought to hold on despite the progressive unraveling of their patients. Had his concern about not becoming the specimen been prophetic? Perhaps we had violated some primitive taboo against cannibalizing brains on that summer afternoon. Without either of us taking notice, perhaps a speck of white substance, it could have passed for a number of things really, had somehow fallen on his wrist. Like Duncan's blood, it might never have washed off. I wondered if years later it was still at him, the source he attributed to the voice he was hearing. Sometimes it seemed as if it were coming from the sink. It would have mimicked his British accent. Kept it up during patient hours because it couldn't hold its tongue, drowning out the dream-tellers on the couch, inviting him to become like the specimen. Eventually that heretical message would have worn him down, like the irresistible flow of water.

Finally after his last patient on a Thursday afternoon, he would have opened his window with a wide view of that historic river, the view that had somehow kept him going when all the dreams were the same. It might have been his version of the Gulf Stream. He might have thought he could hear it flowing, heard it once before, like the running of a tap. It beckoned that someone or something was waiting for him outside. It was time to leave his jar for the other side of the window. He left family and patients behind and a former student from a summer afternoon. Perhaps only that disciple had wondered about an inadvertent spill, a telltale speck that had done just that, went on and on about cutting a brain. He wondered too if there had been a hint of formaldehyde that never washed away.

In my imagined portrayal of Mills's demise, I sensed my own vulnerability, if not to his defenestrated fate, then at least to those voices that would not be silenced, could make themselves heard through the thickest of glass. The whole of a medical career seemed to be cast from his fatal biographic note. Not to become like the specimen would require more than avoidance of contact or an afternoon's diligence in the lab. It wasn't going to be enough to simply cover the blood stains on the surgical drapes with sterile towels, employ frequent glove changes, and reside in that paradoxical remoteness conferred by the operating microscope. I would have to find a way to resist the voices, the ones of the specimens dissected, the patients who had died on my watch, and the relatives for whose grief I had no answer.

REASON

I couched Mills' end, in the words of Camus, more as an act of reason than despair. Others of my colleagues have reached his same conclusion. They would instruct me by the unambiguous nature of their conduct.

One was a former classmate in medical school. If we spoke once in four years, I can't remember. It was almost as if we hadn't met until his name appeared among the obituaries in the *Journal of the AMA*. All the necessary information was there for us to strike up our acquaintance, no matter how belated.

Richard Levy, Temple University Class of '69.

I saw him among fellow classmates streaming through the auditorium doors in the last minutes before the start of another full day of lectures.

Pediatrics.

Perhaps I did have a recollection of him after all. He had always worn a bow tie. He might have been dressing for the part even then.

Suicide.

The picture was complete. For weren't pediatricians reputed to have the second highest rate of suicide among medical specialists? Psychiatrists, I was sure, were the undisputed leaders. When Mills chose to become the specimen it had not been all that unexpected. The practice of empathy is not without risks. But pediatricians? That had been an enigma, at least until Richard Levy and I reminisced. Almost twenty years after graduation, and with the census of Judith's pavilion well established, what his death notice seemed to be saying made perfect sense.

I imagined an endless array of what he would have termed, "the little bastards," parading before him with their colds and earaches. Their parents, particularly the mothers, would have been all the same, room after room, day after day. Posing the same questions, wearing the same outfits, and wiping the same runny noses. Through it all there would have been the crying without end. It was fortunate my classmate had not become a postal worker. Overwhelmed by a never ending supply of catalogs and zip codes, he might have felt compelled to dispatch seven of his coworkers with the help of a mail-order semiautomatic. But he had been schooled in the human body, how it bled, and the grief that attended the dying. He was not about to visit the hospital with an assault rifle, three pistols, and enough ammunition for a protracted siege. He may have simply wandered off, as a child might, and quietly downed enough narcotics for the big sleep. Or if he had added variety to his life since medical school, perhaps he had knotted a full-length tie, one with cartoon characters that could distract his patients, fastened it over a door, and descended to the level of his charges.

Either way, I suspected I knew his reason. It had been his specialty of the well. Normal children, in for a routine checkup or at worst suffering from a self-limiting viral syndrome, had formed the bulk of his pediatric practice. Amid these sanguine throngs, the truly ill had begun to stand apart. Perhaps he even constructed his own tiny pavilion for them, if only in the corner of a playroom. A radiation-like force might have seemed to emanate from these silent children, the ones who didn't make it. Its effect would have been cumulative as a succession of his frail patients withered and died, burying deeper than the never-to-be forgotten loss endured by the parents, beyond that pale. Eventually a sickness of guilt set in and he became haunted by those faces, saw them in each room, until none of his patients seemed well. It was for him the fatal paradox of pediatrics. Behind each door and curtain lurked death, sooner or later, death. Six months or sixty years, it didn't matter. Then, just before the narcotics or the noose, he became convinced that he was responsible for it all. His explanatory note may have tolled a common theme. Something about not deserving to live any longer, not when he couldn't keep his patients with leukemia and brain tumors alive. Alive in the land of youth and vitality he had been overcome by involutional loss. He saw nothing more to live for, and so checked out.

That's what Strange Stanley had done. He was a cardiologist on Miami Beach. His address alone assured his success. He embodied that paradox in medicine that among the ill, extraordinarily bizarre behavior on the part of a physician may pass almost unnoticed. Stanley was as obtuse as his shape. He was all curves. From his face and chin to his abdomen and hips, there was not an angle to be seen. He accentuated this morphology by his habit of never presenting himself full face. It was as if he were constantly being held at bay, someone or something demanding part of his attention. It seemed only natural to address his profile. Even this was fortuitous, for Stanley spat when he spoke. His speech was staccato. His words would remain suspended in the air in front of him as if captured in a high-speed photograph. It was a benefit to that side view: an attempt could be made to read what he had said. But despite this opportunity his ideas frequently failed to coalesce. Instead they would disperse into a fine mist as if intended for the primary though unseen object of his attention. On one occasion when we spoke, Stanley's distraction seemed acute. I became as concerned about him as I was for the patient whom we had been discussing. I phoned the chief of staff at St. Francis Hospital, not to forward a complaint intended to bring sanctions on my colleague, but as an attempt to enroll Stanley in the impaired physicians program. In theory this was designed as a type of community watch, the community being fellow physicians. It provided professional intervention for physicians who showed signs of "cracking up," had gone too far on booze, or had begun taking their own drugs as well as the prescriptions of real and fictitious patients. It acknowledged that there but for the grace of any number of variables, might be any one of us. I thought that Stanley was a doctor in the kind of shape for which that program had been developed. My effort at intervention was, I thought, an act of compassion. For despite his preoccupation, I found something engaging about Stanley as well. It went beyond our mutual forties and our common northeast roots. What we shared may have outweighed what set us apart. And during his occasional lucid intervals he seemed genuinely concerned about his patients. Besides, as everyone agreed, "the man was a real workaholic." That seemed to be the deciding issue in the mind of the chief of staff.

"The guy's strange, no doubt about it. But he's got a waiting room full of patients."

That was it. Since the patients didn't know the difference, why should his aberrations bother us? They took it every time, no matter how sparse the physician's advice or how insulting his comments. As for Strange Stanley, even though most of his colleagues listened to him in disbelief, it wasn't enough to get on the horn to someone with authority and say, "What the hell's up with Stanley?" So instead of bringing him in for a little look-see, he was tolerated, waiting-room-full certified. After all, he was a cardiologist in a geriatric community. Unless all his patients lived, it was unlikely that any medical audit would subject him to special scrutiny. He went on practicing, almost all of his colleagues referring to him as "Strange Stanley." I often wondered what his patients thought of him. Some probably considered him God, as in the joke "my doctor the sun." They did keep his waiting room full, which no doubt supported his delusions. He must have been all right. All the world kept coming back. He was still working as a doctor, admitting patients to two hospitals. Whatever he ordered seemed to get done. People were paying attention. "Yes, Doctor," was their most common response. It was programmed, institutionalized, megalomania. Not quite the halcyon days of fee for service, but still going strong enough to support the likes of Strange Stanley. His ego, which always required a two-seater, wasn't about to draw attention to him now. Not when one of his colleagues drove a Rolls Royce with a license plate on the front that advertised, TONSIL KING. Why should Stanley listen to complainers? "Jealous bastards anyway." He was a workaholic, that was all. There was even an element of self-sacrifice to it. Hell, he probably was up for some medal.

Something must have given way. It certainly wasn't due to pressure from his peers. For whatever reason, just after the eye of Hurricane David had passed, Stanley checked himself into one of the recently renovated Art Deco hotels in South Beach and jumped off the roof.

Maybe the weather had something to do with it, the unusually low barometric pressure. Or as with Mills, perhaps

Stanley's voice of reason had finally prevailed. Who knows if in the midst of those high winds it convinced Stanley he could fly? His system of logic that seemed so idiosyncratic to others may have been working perfectly until the end. It had him check into that hotel just minutes from his home. He could have seen his tiled roof with two palm trees on either side. The hotel would have been the best place to get a good look at the extent of the devastation while most of his patients were still in inland shelters. What he could see from his room might not have been enough. He made his way to the roof to get a panoramic view. With the wind in his face, the sound of it filling his ears, he might have still heard, "They love you, Stanley. Your waiting room is filled even now. Look at them with their *Time* magazines from two years ago and that issue of *People* with an actor's recipe for soufflé next to the picture of his newest impregnated girlfriend."

But Stanley wouldn't have been able to see his office building, the one across from the time and temperature sign. He would have wondered if they were lining up outside to see him, even though the streets were deserted and those traffic lights that were still working simply flashed orange or red. The time sign was blank. He needed to get a better look.

"You can do it, Stan." The wind was still gusting to thirty-five and he knew he could. He didn't even have to flap his arms until his room rushed by and he got to test a theory shared with me by an Iranian surgeon, "They die before they even hit the street. Viscera pull right out from their insertions."

If Stanley had entertained flights of grandeur until his last, and Mills had embraced his fear, reasoning it was time to become like the specimen, then Gordie had discharged his passivity in a final act of violence. Gordie had been our neighbor on one of the man-made islands that extended from the Venetian Causeway linking Miami and Miami Beach. He was a physician's version of the Godfather, as close to a don as a Jewish doctor on Miami Beach could get. He and his family lived within a walled waterfront estate, a separate garage-house guarding the entrance. Beyond an imposing gate, that house seemed to harden under the South Florida sun with an impenetrable glaze. Gordie's eighty-five-year-old father had moved in with them almost a decade before. Three generations living within those walls reinforced the notion of a family enclave under siege. While serving as president of the medical staff at St. Francis, Gordie was at last in character. On one occasion, funds were needed for the hospital's new physician lounge. He rejected soliciting the staff or board members for donations. Instead, at an executive meeting, he whispered in what was his normal speaking tone, "You need some money? We'll make a few calls."

There it was, the long arm on Miami Beach in the late seventies that could reach out to touch someone or call in a favor. But Gordie's influence did not stem from any implied threat. It was a natural consequence of his example by demeanor. He was a gentleman's gentleman, my neighbor and colleague, ten years my senior, and with none of the ambiguities that obscured Strange Stanley. Gordie never seemed distracted. His eyes were sympathetic even in casual greeting. His lips were expectant, pursed in a desire to be of some comfort. Genuine interest separated his, "How are you doing?" from cliché. Gordie wanted to know, and to know him inspired a desire to tell. His light hair seemed destined to be with him for the duration, and his fondness of fishing kept his tan at just the right temperature. I would see him at sundown with his wife and children walking their dog. It was a weimaraner, big and lean. They held onto its leash as if the dog would readily bite. It was the only hint that there might be more to Gordie than his manifest serenity. That dog earned its keep in our affluent neighborhood. Our waterfront homes were within walking distance to one of the poorer sections of Miami, home to the homeless. It was the type of sociological disparity that mimicked an intense weather front, spawning daylight home invasions from the apposition of extremes of wealth and deprivation. There was a sense of imminent danger which inhabited that neighborhood. It could not be dispelled by the comings and goings of gardeners and the drawbridge of the Venetian Causeway, across which derelicts might stroll at will, could not be continually held in its upright position. Perhaps a measure of foreboding had found its way into Gordie, churned beneath his seeming equanimity, was kept on a leash along with his dog. It had tinted his system of logic, not like Strange Stanley's, but with the kind of coloring that only his psychiatrist knew for sure. It had made him a closet depressive, led him to stalk about the house seeking seclusion, kept him brooding in a darkened study with the dog at his side.

His wife and psychiatrist may have suspected that the question that Gordie pondered was no less than the daily dilemma of existence. But he was hardly a candidate for committal. Gordie was a successful nephrologist, in charge of an entire dialysis program, machines, medications, complications. He was the doctor responsible for keeping forty-five patients alive each week. Forty-five human beings looked to him as their link to life-sustaining therapy. It was not the type of medical practice thought to be salutary for a depressive. Just the opposite. None of his patients would ever be cured. Their kidneys would not regenerate and they were not about to gain entry to that list of hopefuls who would be rewarded when some young father on his way to work was killed by a drunk driver. Gordie's patients were attached to their dialysis machines and to him for life. It was just assumed that it would be the end of their lives that would sever the bond.

More than the chronicity of their illness defined Gordie's patients. They were all sophisticates in medical care by virtue of personal experience. They were expert in needle insertion and catheter maintenance. Their familiarity with the composition of the solutions used in their dialysis machines rivaled that of the pharmacists. They had long since lost a sense of mystique when it came to doctors and hospitals. Even as a consultant in neurosurgery I was greeted by most of his patients with more skepticism than gratitude. Whatever respect they still had, they were saving for their soft-spoken nephrologist. He was the one doctor they didn't want to piss off, no matter how much he wished they could. They knew he could pull the plug on them whenever he chose. Otherwise they weren't taking shit from anybody, certainly not from the likes of Strange Stanley. Those who knew him wouldn't let him through the door, let alone allow him to put a stethoscope on their chests. They didn't care how crowded his waiting room was. One even volunteered to her cronies, as they were leashed to their machines, how she had known him for a fraud the first time she had seen him. It was the time she had been admitted with phlebitis and Stanley was seeing the patient in the next bed. "The man never made any sense," was what she said. Wondered how he kept his license, these connoisseurs of medical care, all of them having a love-hate relationship with their dialysis machines. They ended up giving them names and personalities. "She's good to me, but ties me down." Gordie's patients would seldom travel. Without him standing guard, there was no assurance that the dialysis center in the city they were visiting would fulfill their needs.

That was the quality of Gordie's practice even before it changed, before Medicare reimbursements for chronic dialysis were cut back by the government. That set resentment to working both ways. The hospital started looking at dialysis patients as liabilities instead of the cash cows they had once been. As the decreasing funds trickled down to cutbacks and then layoffs, the nurses in the unit made it clear up front who was back in charge. The patients weren't about to take that lying down. It was up to Gordie to pacify both groups, to dissipate amidst the droning of those dialysis machines and his patients' rising urea, the rancor that had developed between the nurses and the long-timers, the ones who had seen it all. Gordie was their only constant, someone both patients and staff could depend upon, the nephrologist with the soft voice, a prince, a savior, and always caring.

Had he unleashed his dog upon that feuding lot perhaps it might have saved him. But that was not his style. He got to brooding more, made worrying a second, full-time profession. Six months before his death, he phoned me at six in the morning. I was scheduled to operate on one of his patients later that day. He told me he couldn't sleep, wanted reassurance that his patient would be all right. I told him it was time for me to do the worrying. I should have done more, maybe asked him how long he hadn't been sleeping because of his patients. Instead my ego-charged response only confirmed that he had reached a wrong number. Whom could he have called, as involved as he was with those forty-five patients he was nurturing on those machines? He was mothering them beyond the scope of the species. The biologic record was only a litter of seven. Perhaps he had kept to that pace because anything less than a full-time commitment would have exposed him to the demon at his heels. It wasn't Strange Stanley's delusion of indispensability. It was a knowledge that his patients were keeping him alive. Theirs were the only voices that could temporarily distract him from the master of his depression. Left to reason in those pensive hours in his study, in calm and dispassionate discourse, Gordie was at a loss to explain his continued existence.

The day came when he stopped trying. He retrieved the handgun that he had ostensibly purchased as a last line of defense in our affluent but embattled neighborhood, polished it with the same care he applied to his stethoscope before listening to the rattles of forty-five dialysis patients each week. Then he fired it into the center of his being, which was not in either of his flanks, the repository of the lifeless vestiges of those failed organs of his charges, but just in front of his right ear, so as to dispatch himself with the decorum and resoluteness and anger befitting his decision.

At the time it was natural to think he had succumbed to his dedication. On the morning his family awoke to the sound of a gun shot, his son was dispatched to our house. It was a Sunday. Perhaps Gordie had chosen the day knowing the lab would be closed. It would have been less disruptive to the program. I have always considered myself fortunate that we were away that weekend. There was nothing I could have done anyway, except wait for the wail of the sirens and then stay clear of the real professionals in the field. I suspect I would have climbed into the ambulance alongside him, pulled what rank I had with that meaningless gesture, as much to get away from the wife and children he had left behind as to complete the necessary prerequisites to pronouncing him dead. I'm grateful that I wasn't there. I can still remember him as the calm mover of communities he had been in that executive committee meeting, and hear his voice more controlled than plaintive on the morning of his patient's scheduled surgery. He has remained my colleague, rather than a mortally wounded victim, with only the miserable irony of his status as a kidney donor still in doubt.

AMPUTATION

What began in Anne's room and carried me against my wishes to the morgue has left me there. The cumulative suicides of my colleagues have not delivered me from that place. As I seek to depart by measured steps, I pass a severed foot. Its owner-amputee lies on a higher Pavilion floor recovering from her recent surgery. Edith Small was a 1967 version of a homeless lady. Not that she lived out of a shopping cart or talked incessantly to her two sweaters. It was more a sense that she didn't exist beyond the hospital. She and her diabetes had settled in there. Her insulin shots marked the change of shift and break times for the nurses. They set their watches by each injection, as if the needle were a watchman's key, and her body the most remote station on their rounds. A gangrenous foot confined her to her bed and fixed our views of one another. As I stood below that foot, her eyes were of necessity downcast. From my vantage point her face was like a cliff, something I would have to climb to gain her attention. The first obstacles were her jaw and turned-down lips that seemed to have a cragged edge at either side. From there her high and rounded cheekbones offered very little hold. Had we been face to face I could have seen those eyes better. Instead they were sunken below the overhang of her brows. I spoke mainly to her lashes, flickering twigs set below her whitish hair.

The room that Edith and her foot shared was in Philadelphia's Episcopal Hospital. Episcopal had remained unchanged from the First World War. Just to get there was to go back in time. Lehigh Avenue was still brick paved. Recessed trolley tracks offered only the illusion of an available smooth surface. At any of the endless untimed traffic lights, a procession of black Model Ts could be imagined crossing by. A young boy in a flannel cap might just as well be offering the latest edition of the Inquirer with news from the front. The hospital seemed just behind the lines. The lighting was natural. Large storied windows on open staircases bracketed otherwise darkened halls. The smoke from nearby factories cast a battlefield pall upon the scene. Inside Edith's room, there was an uneasy truce. Upon entering I felt obliged to acknowledge both her and that foot. At one end was Edith's head, never complaining and always pleasant despite her confinement. Her reception cheered us on, new doctors on rotation, just arrived to "over there." How many like us had she known before? But the foot was sullen and menacing. A tent-like metal frame protected it from the painful weight of the sheets. "Touch me and it's bad luck," was the message it implied. There was an odor, off-sweet, some unfinished business before it could be spring again. The trenches of the struggle between Edith and her foot were defined by the folds of the bedclothes. The gangrenous foot claimed territory by virtue of its example, the sullen decay it displayed from her heel toward her toes. Perhaps in years long since past, a suitor had cradled in respectful passion that first step to his desired goal. Now it lay decomposing like the rotting apple on Gregor Samsa's back. The ulcer demanded its imperative. Edith's surgeon, our clinical mentor, was prepared to accede. Dr. Kressler's plan was to amputate not only the foot, but the leg as well, to just below the knee, and put an end to that deadly stalemate.

I would have none of that surrender; would-be doctor, too short a time at the front to have seen the inevitable. I was concerned with my own appendages, averse to the thought of cutting off abilities before they had time to develop. Her leg was not to be discarded for lack of effort. I set out along with my fellow student, Rick Fitzgibbons, to prove that surgery would not be necessary. Fitz was West Point material. He had the honest face of Irish America. His hairline peaked above the center of his forehead as if he were already leading a charge. His eyes were wide set to protect the flanks, but there wasn't a moment of suspicion or guarding about him. He was still in the reconnoitering stage. The unanswerable questions of existence would come later. Not that he was naive, merely accepting. Why not a congressional appointment to the academy for this son of a Philadelphia Democrat? Granted; had it not been for his uneven gait, the lasting march of a childhood necrosis of the hip. Perhaps it explained his own resolve to save that leg. The alphabetical determination of our Fitzgibbons-Flitter assignments had made us constant companions. We could have been cops, partners, as we rode to whatever satellite hospital we had been assigned. We were both bachelors, with none of the responsibilities that occupied our married classmates. Any serious relationship had to pass muster with Fitz. It was the job. Who else had been there when he appeared at the doorway of the labor room during our obstetrics rotation and announced his patient's crowning achievement with a feeble, "Help?" But it was Fitz who held me to the sailboat in the Schuylkill River with my shoulder dislocated after we had capsized. We were the two officers assigned to Edith Small and we would have her walk again. Our idea was to apply insulin-soaked dressings to the wound. We proposed it might alter the metabolic needs of those dying tissues at a local level. The dressings were to be changed three times a day, along with what was euphemistically called debridement. We would cut away the dead and purulent tissue, trim the hardened edges of the wound with suture scissors. Edith endured the pain as this battle raged not entirely remote from her sensibilities. We envisioned saving the foot and did not exclude an early Nobel prize for medicine.

At first, because of our care and attention during our time at the front, the foot seemed salvageable. It was as if the tide of battle had turned. Pink traces of healing granulation tissue broke out to surround the margins of the defect that had once been a no-man's-land. It seemed we had thwarted some malicious intent, the had-her-by-a-toe evil that wanted to drag her down to a nursing home. It had envisioned her as a veteran in a wheelchair, with her meals and life on a tray. If she were lucky she might have a view of a tree, stare at it while she waited for the mail that never came and tried to forget that she was alone. Fitz and I celebrated our seeming victory and shared our enthusiasm with Dr. Kressler. The improvement was palpable and instructive. A clinical problem that had weeks before seemed amenable only to cutting away, now proclaimed healing and recovery. It was all so simple, an intuitive breakthrough that had awaited our presence. We had merely dispatched those insulin dressings as reinforcements. Since it would be three years before Dr. Kressler's stroke that left him hemiplegic and aphasic at forty-five, and his heart attack that stilled him forever at forty-eight, he was generous in his opinion. He encouraged us to continue, but added a note of caution.

"Boys, perhaps what you are seeing here is primarily the benefit of frequent dressing changes. You might think about a control on a similar patient in which you use saline instead of insulin. The results might be equally salutary."

His suggestions were noted. If anything we thought they amounted to only a slight delay in the ultimate prize, though what he went on to say, in his seasoned directness, made us uneasy.

"By the way, who's going to tend to this wound when you finish your rotation next week?"

There it was, the gauntlet of "Let's see what kind of troopers you are." He knew the schedule of medical students. Free time, particularly during clinical rotations, would be at a premium. Would we visit her at night, after completing our newest assignments? Hunt up instruments and bandages, and work out the insulin availability? At first that's just what we did. And during the day the floor nurses applied new dressings in our absence. But they were unable to debride the wound. There were nights when we were assigned to remain at the University Hospital and couldn't see her at all. Our classmates who followed us to Episcopal could not be convinced to continue the project. They seemed more interested in the prospect of assisting in their first amputation. Whatever improvement had occurred seemed to halt, and then retreat. Even Edith seemed to lose interest in what we were doing. When we were able to return to her room, she seemed to leave us alone with her foot. It became unclear who or what we were trying to save.

In the end we all surrendered to the attrition of that campaign. Edith's surgery was scheduled and done and she was discharged to somewhere.

But the memory of Edith could not be amputated from my sensibilities or my frame of reference. Decades later, I cannot hold a patient's foot in examination to feel for a pulse, request the ankle to be flexed against my resistant grasp, or draw a key beneath the sole, without first taking care to avoid the area of ulceration on Edith's Episcopal foot, the tread of the homeless, lest I reach into some black hole in my past and become part of the putrefaction and defeat of the victories that are not meant to be.

FRIENDSHIP

I held no ill feelings toward my fellow students whose rotation at Episcopal had followed ours. No doubt they were involved in their own projects and viewed Dr. Kressler's decision to amputate as a clinical imperative. It wasn't the first time I felt more closely allied to my peers through schedule than philosophy. Even in college, there was the sense that my classmates and I were not all brethren in spirit. But this was medical school, certainly a few of them had to view life as I did, see the humor and pathos and the absurdity of so much of what we were going through to become doctors. Of the few who did, Steve was to become my closest friend.

We first met in the cafeteria during the second week of our freshman year. We recognized each other among the three-to-eleven hospital shift despite the separation of our alphabetically derived group assignments. Flitter and Fitzgibbons would save each other later. This was the chance meeting of Flitter and Weinreb, class of '65 and '56 respectively. He cracked me up, something he said about the horseshit of what we were supposed to memorize, and how after a while his vision blurred as he struggled to interpret what was staring back through the microscope from his histology slide. Maybe it was my laughter, or something I said that sent out acknowledgment and understanding. We had made contact even before his famous touch.

To this day I remember his hands. His fingers were thin and surprisingly long, well suited to the purpose of gesture and touch. They were not the hands of a stonecutter, no marble angel would mark his home, but hands that had lived themselves, could tell their own stories. The skin was seamless. Steve might have been a surgeon without gloves, perhaps an ophthalmologist, eyes calling those hands to their delicate hue. They were hands that had not labored beyond reason through the whole of his life. They had typed his submissions to the Dartmouth student newspaper during his undergraduate years. They had retrieved volumes from The Yale Law Library while he earned his LLD. And after graduation they steadied clients at a Manhattan law firm until this Brooklyn boy who had touched the façade of the Ivy League discovered he wasn't at home on Madison Avenue. They accompanied him then at night to Long Island University, where he earned a master's degree in psychology. And during the day they earned their keep in their most dramatic form: he had become an actor. He told me he had worked with Julie Harris and I always pictured him opposite her in *Moon of the Misbegotten*. But I never found his gestures to be acting.

When he spoke, it was the opposite of Strange Stanley. Steve would hold my attention physically, with his gaze and with one of those hands on my arm. He said that no one touched any more. That was in 1961, before AIDS and herpes, before masked and gloved rescue workers, donning hazmat overalls, had begun to wander through the wreckage of a disaster as if they were the victims. From his small face his eyes seemed to point, elf-like. His smile was for all reasons. When we discovered the absurdity of a particular lab exam, it was genuinely funny. But when confronted with a patient's suffering, Steve's bemused expression revealed his philosophy. His wonderment at the indifference of the universe knew no bounds. His hairline was receding like Mills'. Perhaps there is something to an exposed forehead that invites the discipline of psychiatry. For Steve, medical school was another way station on the path to that most cerebral of specialties. It was to be his last frontier and where we would diverge. Our mutual fascination with the brain was leading us to different conclusions. The paradox of Steve's choice was that his manipulation of that structure would preclude touch. As for me, I would try to re-assemble within neurosurgery the broken toys of my father's offhand remark, "The boy breaks everything he touches."

Steve was forty while I was twenty-one. We formed an exclusionary odd couple. He was divorced from what we suspected as nonsense by virtue of his experience, and I, perhaps by intuition. And I wish he were still here.

Medical school was a struggle for us both. It wasn't that we were underachievers who shouldn't have been there in the first place. Our desperation was founded in the emphasis for memorization. Our preference for the abstract was being suffocated by the concrete nature of what we were required to learn. Steve used to say that any idiot could get through medical school. There was a mnemonic for everything. "On Old Olympus Towering Top A Finn And German Vault And Hop." That's how we memorized the cranial nerves, long before Nelson Graves graphically demonstrated their dysfunction. We were back in nursery school where the meter of our recitations was a far cry from Dylan Thomas. And there was no way to approach insertions and origins as if reading *Crime and*

Punishment. It never occurred to us in our intellectual rebelliousness that when a patient can't breathe or is hemorrhaging, what's needed is less a poet than some good old boy who has aced the rote. We looked at each other when the rest of the class was paying attention to the biochemistry professor, "Bones" Hamilton, as he explained the best way to wash glass beakers. Apparently several washes with a small amount of water is preferable to a single brimming effort. Steve and I dealt with our own stress by noting the coping mechanisms of others. We compared our observations regarding which of our classmates seemed close to breaking, kept a list of impending casualties. In part, that is how we got through, how we kept ourselves from breaking.

Our attention was first drawn to a classmate who had appeared at orientation wearing a white jacket. While the rest of us seemed to have not yet left college, he was dressed for office hours. He was a foreshortened version of Oliver Hardy, complete with mustache. Although he had been uniformed for the part, he was gone by the end of the first semester. Before he left, Steve and I would see him each night in the histology lab as we tried to make sense of our slides. He would appear as if from nowhere, walk across that otherwise empty room and force open one of the six-foot windows. He would extend his head and neck outside, presumably to check the weather. As we watched, what he seemed to be attempting was much more. It was a ritual of partial exit and one which diffused our own ambivalence. He enacted the extent to which we would have wished to quit that place, sought freedom out that window. But we had chosen that course. It was the lab, our microscopes, and cadaver that held us there. Short of experimenting with our colleague's apparent technique, there was nothing to do but get on with it, back to our slides and rote. With that our alter ego would return inside, close the window and disappear. Years later I still can't part my bedroom drapes to see if it's snowing, without wanting to issue a qualifier to my wife: *It's not that I want to leave,* remembering the almost-doctor who had kept those nightly vigils off Broad Street, where the buildings and noise made it impossible to detect anything more subtle than a blizzard or torrential downpour.

Our watchfulness took a solemn turn. We had placed on our list of impending casualties one of the youngest students in our class. He had been admitted after only two years in college, and his frail and boyish face spoke of grades in high school he may have skipped as well. But his Phi Beta Kappa key conferred no protection in our growing-up world. He began to write cryptic messages on the auditorium blackboard before the start of our morning lectures, the content of these inscriptions beyond the rhyme and reason of our subjects. Each professor would erase what had been written, dismissing it as just another student prank. It didn't seem to matter who the author was or what he was trying to say. As the first lecture of the day began we would all resume furiously writing our own notes. It wasn't until the Monday morning when we heard that he had shot himself, that we considered his text more carefully. But by then it was too late. The image of his handwriting, a delicate and legible script whose meaning I had ignored, returned to haunt me. In the end his message was one of irony. If any of us were ill or in need of help, it was unlikely to be addressed within that setting. There hadn't been a lecture about helping each other.

The attrition continued, fortunately without further suicides. Steve and I continued to confront the mindless repetition through humor. Our bond was secure in the inexhaustible material at hand. We remained closest during the basic science years, before Weinreb and Flitter were dispatched to different clinical rotations. Once before the first part of National Board exams, he returned to school with a woman. He said that they were married and that he thought it might help him study. Whether it helped or didn't, I never knew. She left before the end of that term and the next series of examinations. Steve and I were alone again, with only each other to confirm our frame of reference. But in that sharing I had no doubt of my impressions and opinions. Steve recognized the absurd as well when one of our classmates participated in a postmortem dissection of his own grandfather.

Steve didn't change much. Just before we graduated he placed a letter in all our mailboxes. It was about our professor of psychiatry with whom he had become friendly. They had played tennis twice a week. Steve had discovered by accident a letter that our professor, his friend, had written in response to a request for a recommendation. It portrayed Steve as a candidate unlikely to ever settle down, always going on to the next intellectual or professional challenge. It ended with an expression of regret that unfortunately he could not recommend Steve for a position in a psychiatry training program. The professor used the initial "R" in his name. Steve concluded his letter revealing this betrayal, by suggesting that the mystery of the R. had been solved. It stood for rattler.

After graduation, Steve served his internship at Chestnut Hill Hospital. He told me he had hidden in the bathroom every time a cardiac arrest was called. From there he went on to complete a psychiatry residency at Michael Reese in Chicago. He explained to me that they had a little problem with him there.

"The purpose of the program was to make you sick, but I went in that way." Our professor had been wrong. Steve never left psychiatry, never found that discipline wanting. He married a woman twenty-three years his junior and they moved to California. He had a storefront practice in Berkeley. We kept in touch over the years. Mostly I would call when writing a piece for the local medical journal to confirm a reference he had made years before to Kierkegaard or Yevtushenko at a time when otherwise our study was at the level of nursery rhymes.

I visited Steve once when I traveled to San Francisco for a meeting. We promised that it wouldn't be another decade before we met again. It was only two years later that I received a note from his wife, a line or two that said, *I know you would want to know, Steve died of stomach cancer* on such and such a date. And that was all, his voice was stilled, no more laughter or insights, no more touching across continents just by a mutually understood reference to the insanity that we had endured.

He was fifty-two when he died.

I sometimes think about his daughter, only an infant as I sat on the floor of their apartment, and avoided watching her breast-feed. I wonder if her humor and gentleness are Steve's, her intelligence and untiring curiosity, keeping him alive in his fifty-percent genetic fate.

SYMMETRY

The feature I would have most likely noticed in Steve's daughter would have been the shape of her head. If I had held her for a moment, I would have enclosed that crown as much to feel the symmetry as the softness, acknowledging the journey my own hands had made since Steve and I had first met. By then my hands had become an extension of my memory. As I cradled her head, it would have been Jorge Rivera that I was holding.

Jorge had redefined for me the term normocephalic. Before I had cared for him it had simply referred to the unremarkable shape of a patient's head. Would that it had retained that calm exterior. But its symmetry was lost forever, early in my neurosurgical practice, in the sharpening contours of Jorge's head. A boat-shaped appearance was how his young parents had described it when he was only six months old. It wasn't because they had both been in the second wave of refugees from Mariel to Key West. To these Miami Cubans that voyage was far behind. It had been made so by their reception. They were being absorbed into the transplanted ethnic community of their countrymen with a practiced ease. Even their name, "Rivera," had a coastal serenity that suggested they were almost home. If little Jorge had some sharpness to him, that could be smoothed out in time.

"Not to worry," promised their pediatrician, who was himself doing fine, without a hint of depression over this relatively rare anomaly. "I'll get you to a neurosurgeon who can fix it."

"There's no implication regarding your son's development," I explained to Jorge's parents. They had a handsomeness about them that offered no hint of their child's imperfection. The father was blue collared and tan with a carefully trimmed mustache that seemed designed to belie his own baby-like face. Jorge's mother possessed a dark Latin beauty that even without extensive makeup would have been striking. Their parental concern defied stereotype. It was universal.

"His condition is called premature cranial synostosis. The suture lines in the skull where growth continues until the age of two have fused before their time."

In my own mind, a resonant thespian voice was critical of anything before its time. It was difficult for me to know how much of my explanation Jorge's parents were following. It wasn't entirely a question of language. Their anxiety at hearing their child cast as somehow different may have been magnified by their not yet complete assimilation.

"There is an operation that can be done. By removing strips of bone in the skull, new growth areas can be created. This will allow his head to assume a more normal shape as he gets older. From what you say, he's been eating well and his examination shows no other problems. The reason for putting him through this, and there are risks, is for the sake of appearance."

I didn't tell them about the likely moniker that other kids would mercilessly apply while moving in for the kill.

"Hey boat head, can you play? It's called, 'Carry me home.'"

I certainly thought it was reasonable to proceed. If there were any drawbacks it was Jorge's age. His potential for new bone growth would be diminished as he grew older. The sooner the operation could be performed, the more likely it would accomplish its goal. I explained to them in greater detail the risks, described the possibility of infection, of damage to the surface of the brain, and the occasional need for further surgery. I included the last as a somewhat vague reminder that unforeseen complications can occur. It was prophetic.

They gave me permission to take their son, their only son, their baby boy who other than having a somewhat strange shape to his head was perfectly normal, to the operating room. There an intravenous line was inserted in a vein in his arm, he was placed under a general anesthetic, and a tube was inserted in his trachea. I shaved the fine down from his scalp and saw his baby's head as if he had not yet been born. He was anointed with iodine and the surgical drapes placed upon him.

I hesitated for a moment, the scalpel poised above the dark blue ink with which I had marked his forehead just behind the hairline. I was anticipating another interval of time, this from deed to consequence. It wouldn't be noted in seconds, but in some other measure, that irreducible pause between the incision of a scalp and the appearance of blood. It was what was required to pass from surprise to outrage. For nature intended to protect us first from so-called blunt trauma. The layers of our scalps are suited to catch a rock or perhaps a branch and cast either back more in derision than offense. But between blade and blood is the body's disbelief. Perhaps it is the purity of the cut that dismisses all matter as inconsequential. A scalpel can strike a line on underlying bone like a contrail at dusk. It cuts through the millennia of survival's refinement and violates the inviolable. For a surgeon there is one thing more between that cause and effect. It is the notion of, "Look what you have done." Then that moment of contemplation is gone, dismissed in the momentum of the rushing blood. Even the name "scalpel" revealed the root of my intent.

I incised Jorge's scalp from ear to ear along his hairline as Anne's had been when last I saw her. His child's loss of blood demanded control under penalty of transfusion. All went well. With attention to detail I set upon creating new sutures in his underlying bone. During one of the cuts I nicked the dura, the covering of the brain, with the rotating blade of the high-speed drill. There was no damage to the brain itself, but at the defect, drops of pristine fluid appeared. It was spinal fluid, which bathed the brain and lay beneath the membrane I had cut. At the time it inspired no alarm. I completed the remaining passes of the drill through Jorge's compliant skull. The edges of his bone drew apart as if some new life form were about to emerge from a rendered shell. Instead only drops of fluid appeared and from just one point. I had no doubt that it would stop. There was no bleeding. I covered the tiny defect in the dura with a small strip of foam-like gel, more than enough to form a seal. I reapproximated the scalp as a child's puzzle, margins of sun and sky returned to their proper place. Jorge appeared at peace below his full white head dressing, a roundness to his future now. He awoke and quickly passed from irritability to hunger and then to play. His mother held him in a rocker by the crib as his father shook my hand.

Before he left the hospital I changed his dressing. The incision was fine. There was no redness by the sutures or tenderness to the touch. But underneath the scalp there was a bogginess, almost a wave-like sense to the fluid that seemed somewhat more than I would have anticipated. I recalled the instant the drill had whined its excess fervor. That was why there was fluid there, and I still thought it would heal.

Ten days later, with Jorge and his parents in my office, instead of there being less fluid, there was more. There was a tenseness to it, a kind of arrogance of station. It knew it had me. Otherwise he was doing well. His parents just wanted to know about the swelling, about when it would go down. It was time to share my concern. I explained that perhaps the leak was ongoing. The emphasis was less on the drill that had been in my hands than on a membrane that wasn't healing as it should. My remaining hope was for the restorative power of Jorge's youth. Perhaps that could win the day, despite what I had done, and dismiss that fluid with its vital mandate. After one more week, they didn't have to ask. Attention was being drawn to Jorge's head because of its consistency now more than its shape. I didn't want to consider what his new nickname might be, and he couldn't wear a cap for the rest of his life. As the surgeon responsible for giving him new sutures, attempting to improve on the ones nature had provided, I was now responsible for the unintended side effect of my efforts. At first I hoped that additional surgery would not be necessary. For the next week I applied pressure dressings. They left indentations on his forehead but had no effect upon the fluid. I prescribed a drug that inhibited his body's production of spinal fluid. The scalp remained tense. Finally the need for a second operation seemed undeniable. The relentless pressure of the fluid, fueled by the ongoing growth of his child's brain, would not permit that leak to stop. I succumbed to what I may have known all along but refused to admit. The longest way was going to be the shortest. I met with his parents once again to explain why he needed more surgery. I planned to suture a patch over that now well-established point of escape, seal the breach in the wall of the cold war I had been waging. It was, in retrospect, what I should have done as soon as I had laid down that errant drill.

Once again Jorge's parents watched their baby disappear behind closed doors. The patch worked perfectly. The wound healed and his scalp approximated his skull with a fluidless seal. At the time I just considered it a two-for-one special. All was well that ended well. Particularly after the two-year statute of limitations for malpractice had expired. Then I was no longer in dread of receiving a registered letter hand-delivered to the office by two Sheriff's deputies, dispatched in case I were to put up a struggle while signing the receipt. I wouldn't have to feel the blood draining out of me for a change as I read the bill of particulars, alleging that everything I had done from start to finish was negligent, despite the fact that by then the shape of Jorge's head was unremarkable. No attorney would entice some bastard from Yale to take a bus ride down to Florida and testify against me for the fee.

Instead of deputies with a notice of intent, there were Christmas cards with handwritten expressions of gratitude, about how the whole family thought of me often and wanted the best for me and my family at that special time of the year. It was pediatrics, the well specialty. I could think about Jorge growing up without the stigma of a misshapen skull, in part because of what I had done, the work of my hands.

Until a Thursday afternoon when my secretary told me there was a Mrs. Rivera on the line. It was Jorge's mother. She was hysterical and cried into the phone something about her baby. Jorge had been playing with his older sister and a friend and they had come running, told her Jorge was turning blue.

For some reason she had thought of calling me first. Wondered if it had something to do with his operations? I could hear children calling Jorge's name in the background.

"What was he doing?" I asked, thinking perhaps it was a seizure.

"They were just playing and Jorge had a balloon. I heard a pop and then his sister started to scream."

"Call an ambulance. Take him to the hospital and call me from there."

Jorge was never admitted to that hospital. They pronounced him dead in the emergency room. I received the message later that day. The cause of death was still unknown. An autopsy was scheduled for the next morning. As I drove to the morgue for Jorge's last procedure I thought about what might have happened. I kept hearing what his mother had told me.

"They were playing. Jorge had a balloon, and I heard a pop."

The morgue was in a trailer attached to Jackson Memorial Hospital. There were cadavers in the hallway waiting to be admitted into their own freezer compartments. The sounds of the compressors created a general Judgment Day din. I had met the pathologist once before, had watched him perform an autopsy on a trauma patient I thought we should have saved. I told him what I knew of the history. How I knew the patient, had operated on him twice, suspected he may have choked on something. The pathologist went right to it, incised Jorge's perfect neck. There was no bleeding. He opened the trachea slowly, in a pace that didn't make any difference. There it was, a fragment of a bright balloon. It was Jorge's one-in-a-million chance. Stop the entire nation at any one moment. How many children are playing with balloons, bouncing them off of each other's heads, watching them hit the ceiling and calling for their mothers to get them down? It happens so often that the mothers tie the balloons to their children's wrists, harmless as they are.

Except for Jorge's, the child who had survived two surgeries. He had put his lips against his balloon and then opened his mouth. The feel of it had been strange. He inhaled the odor of the latex as he looked at the colored light from the lamp on the other side of his balloon. He heard the pop and then felt something strange. He wanted to call Mommy, but nothing would come out, and then nothing would go in. Not that he didn't try his best, until it seemed like he was falling asleep.

I shook hands with the pathologist and left that place. But since that morning, for me "normocephalic" has always meant balloon-shaped.

PART FOUR

The Vista

INFLUENCE

Would that Jorge's balloon had done just that, drifted to the ceiling of that playroom and then higher, taken him and me out of our morgues, to a place where there is no death. It cannot be. Instead I am borne in an elevator to the uppermost part of Judith's pavilion. I resist the urge to say, "Eight, please, Hampton."

The doors open on the highest floor of the Miami Heart Institute, the template of my memories, to a spacious table-filled room that is cafeteria by day and meeting room by night. Three of the walls serve rich windowed views of South Florida. To the west the skyline of downtown Miami reaches upward. Miami Beach and Key Biscayne beckon to the south. To the north sprawl Hollywood and Fort Lauderdale. The closest building of equal stature is Mount Sinai Hospital. It is within walking distance across Alton Road. The two institutions keep a watchful eye on one another, competition being what it is. My attention is always drawn to the canopied windows of the VIP eighth floor at Sinai. It was to one of those privileged rooms that my friend and colleague, Jacob Frank, was untimely transferred.

Jacob also lived on our island off the Venetian Causeway. Even with Gordie gone, almost all of the medical specialties were represented. A walk along its perimeter drive might easily lead to a curbside consultation, assuming another physician ventured from behind his mechanized gates or occlusive shrubbery. None of my colleagues was more willing to chat than Jacob, the respected chairman of the radiation oncology department at Mount Sinai. He had emigrated from South Africa. The formality of his speech, a characteristic King's English, was softened by a menschlekite soul and served him well in dealing with his Miami Beach patients. They came to him hoping for a miracle at "Sinai." What they sought was but a slight delay of their inevitable fate, and through Jacob's powerful radiation units many were granted such a stay.

Jacob had been perfectly cast. His chest and shoulders were broad, and his voice was deep. Wild locks of graying hair and a beard completed the sense that if required he would wrestle with the grim reaper on behalf of his patients. He was Moses and David to his flock. They gathered round him with their myelomas and prostate cancers, tumors of the breast and skin. Their bodies were tanned and wrinkled as if they had spent forty years on their morning beaches, in prayerful exercise and religious walks of flight. They were his survivors. What added to his mystique was that many of their conditions, rapidly fatal in younger patients, behaved more benignly in octogenarians. Jacob didn't have to extend a life all that long to become a hero and inspire a one-upmanship donation to his department. It was only money. To the hospital board it was manna from heaven. Jacob converted the funds to equipment that could accelerate particles as fast as any unit in the south. Sinai became a nuclear power with the acquisition of its own reactor, used to produce isotopes for nuclear medicine. The secluded wood-paneled offices in his department proliferated. Through it all, Jacob remained accessible in spirit and time. Mere mortals, who had reached neither his physical nor material state, were inspired by his vitality and experienced a balm in his presence.

Perhaps that was why word of his heart attack was received with a combination of sadness and something more. There was the intimation of one's own vulnerability. If the likes of Jacob could be stricken, who among us was safe? His recovery was slow, his walks around the island more invalid than regal. When we came upon each other he assured me his recovery was on schedule. I remembered the first summer we met. I had just joined the staff at Sinai and was renting a single-story, two-bedroom house across the street from the waterfront homes that drew the attention of the Circle Line tourists cruising Biscayne Bay. I had been introduced to Jacob at the hospital, and he asked me where I was living. He offered to help me furnish that house from a store of old belongings in his attic. The day of the move, he had carried a table and chairs down the steps by himself and had loaded them into the back of his station wagon before I arrived. He had ignored my request to wait for me so that I could lend a hand, or arrange for someone else to do it. Jacob's suburban hauler, turned *Grapes of Wrath* in that driveway, struck me as somehow snowbound. It was the association I made with rare physical exertion. When I was still in grade school a friend of my father's had collapsed and died while pushing a car that was buried in the snow. That was my first clinical instruction on what middle-aged men shouldn't do. Almost a decade after Jacob's generosity of material and effort that lesson seemed once more to be borne out. When our chance meeting occurred during his recuperation under the South Florida sun, I thought of Jacob as less stranded than floundering. The spasm of his coronary arteries had left him with damaged sails, at a disadvantage should ill winds blow his way.

Which is just what occurred two years later as he drove his compact car to North Miami Beach, a statement in itself of his reapportioned priorities. Jacob had been on one of his semi-weekly pilgrimages, in flight from the changing economics of health care. Oversupply and dwindling reimbursement had overtaken the hospital as much as his clogged arteries were closing in on him. Medicine devoted to diseases of the rich, which had brought a gold rush fortune to so many on that gold coast, had begun to feel the pinch. Jacob was taking a leadership role among the hospital-based physicians. He had agreed to see patients in Sinai's satellite facility so that his department and the hospital would not lose paying customers to institutions in Hollywood and Fort Lauderdale or even West Palm Beach. He was going to where the patients were, those retirees who had chosen to forego Collins Avenue and Bal Harbor for the more northerly golf course condominiums. If they were no longer living in Miami Beach, it was time to take Mecca to the disciples. Jacob, along with internists and surgeons, was trying to land a few of the remaining paying patients to keep his practices and Sinai going a little bit longer.

Jacob's accident was a circus mismatch, his compact car struck by a Lincoln filled with teenagers riding their parents' largesse. In that one instant he was transformed from doctor to victim, restrained in the wreckage by the metal and steering wheel impressed upon his chest. Until he was extracted, traffic was drawn to a halt, like a propagating blood clot on 163rd Street, past miles of strip malls with bagel emporiums and golf shops, kitchen and bathroom accessories, notaries public, shoe stores, delicatessens, and eventually an upscale mall with a Macy's. He had become a casualty of the last American frontier, land developed for small business entrepreneurs who would stake their claims until they couldn't compete with mail-order catalogues or superstores. In Florida they were converging from both coasts, headed to an economic Promitory Point where the weight of a megalopolis might just cause the peninsula to sink. Jacob had come a long way from South Africa.

The news of his accident traveled throughout the hospital as if 911 had been broadcast over the speaker system. Jacob had been transported to Sinai and was admitted to the intensive care unit. He had sustained fractured ribs and a contusion of the lung. Those findings were sufficient to raise an element of concern in the mind of any physician. Who didn't know that after most heart attacks the heart would neither forget or forgive? Jacob's would be weighted down with scar tissue that could turn even a minor assault or stress, a swell that would otherwise be ridden with ease, into a rogue wave that could capsize a thirty-foot sloop. The scene was set, Jacob in ICU, his breathing limited by pain coming from those fractured ribs. There had been no changes in his EKG thus far. It seemed as if he would get through his injuries. I saw him sleeping there as I visited a post-op patient. His face was bruised, *our Jacob*. It gave him a frail appearance which in that instant made me grateful that we had a hospital with nurses and doctors who could take over for him when he needed a little respite. They'd help him with his pain until he could be on his feet again. And he had improved by the next day. His breathing was easier, and he was able to sit up for a few minutes before the pain returned. He had asked for the head of his bed to be lowered then. But he greeted the trauma surgeon and the cardiologist with the same message. "Ready for transfer."

Transfer to "Eight Main" was the unquestioned implication. On that floor each room had its own refrigerator and was decorated more like a hotel than a hospital. The hallways were wallpapered, lunch catered, and the dinner menus à la carte. Having made his request, Jacob had pronounced himself fit for such a transfer. A radiation oncologist, all his expertise in rads and fields, as unfamiliar with trauma patients as he was with post myocardial infarctions, he awaited the certain acquiescence of his colleagues. They didn't disappoint him. Both the surgeon and the cardiologist agreed with their doctor-patient's plan of treatment. In the political climate of the hospital, Jacob was to be their friend at the top, insurance in uncertain times. He would be their voice to the board when the big crunch came, protect them from the cross-bay university that sought to expand its turf into the community medical center. Their professional expertise couldn't dispel their concerns about that or about the continuing flight of their patients northward. They wrote Jacob's transfer orders as if filling out an RSVP for an exclusive affair. It was transfer to Eight Main, effected less than forty-eight hours after this bear of a man had been tossed about in his toy car like a toy himself. He probably would have been killed if it were not for his seat belt and shoulder harness. The paperwork was completed and the ICU nurses wheeled him out of that unit to his private room. A little influence in the system never hurt. His room was already filled with flowers from his admirers, former patients, and respectful colleagues. He may have even felt better through the afternoon in those brighter surroundings. He had the curtains opened to take in the ocean view. His goal was to be out of bed and in a chair after dinner.

Almost without warning, hardly enough time for the volunteer who was refilling Jacob's water pitcher to ask, "What's wrong?", Jacob changed. His face, despite the fresh bruises, showed a pallor she had never seen before. Nor had she heard breathing like that. There was nothing rhythmic or hypnotic in its irregularity. "How could this be?" she thought. "We've just been talking." She reached for the nurses' call bell, which on that floor had been more frequently depressed for the Grey Poupon than any medical complaint. But now it was for a patient who was dying, and not just any patient, but Jacob himself. She ran down the hallway past the candy and newspaper cart and came upon the charge nurse. The nurse had planned to answer the call light as soon as she had finished going over the vacation schedule with an LPN. She thought the light in Jacob's room was probably a request to turn down the air-conditioning or perhaps close the drapes. But when she saw how gray the *gray lady* was she knew it was for something else, and rushed past her down the hall. She saw the perspiration on his face and sensed the cold in his neck as she sought his pulse, knew then he was in shock. She wouldn't remember picking up the phone and crying to the operator, "Code blue, Eight Main."

This time Jacob's condition was in fact being broadcast throughout the hospital. Although to most of the trained ears hearing that alarm, Eight Main did not complete the association. Under normal circumstances Eight Main conveyed none of the ominous implications that seemed inescapable when the maternity or pediatric floors were announced. What scenario could justify a death on either of those units? But when the VIP floor was the specified location of a code blue, there was the possibility of a less disturbing event. An inference might be drawn that a major benefactor was about to receive the hospital's last rites. It wasn't unusual for Sinai to be chosen as the place for terminal care. Nothing ostentatious, but the surroundings did lend themselves to conferences with a family attorney and Sinai's location offered a more convenient getaway from the dying for tennis or golf than those awful nursing homes in

North Miami with their smells and their tenants stacked in the hallways in a final holding pattern that never seemed to abate. A family doctor could be just that, available to dispense tranquilizers or sedatives to a spouse or grown child. Usually within weeks after the funeral a major bequest to the hospital's trust foundation completed the admission and discharge. There was no reason to think on this day it was anything else but business as usual. After all, Jacob was still in ICU, would most likely be there for another two to three days. They'd make sure he was stable before thinking about moving him out. But the trauma surgeon and cardiologist who had sent him there were unable to ignore their worst fears. As the house officers who had code beepers responded without knowing who the patient was, they were calling the nursing station.

"Not Jacob, I hope?"

The answer left them unable to believe their bad luck, not to mention Jacob's. "Shit. Son of a bitch."

Both of them arrived just about the same time, quickly glanced at each other, knowing it was in the fire now, with only the other as an ally. Events had proceeded beyond them. The momentum of Jacob's arrest was being played out by the book. The chief medical resident made the team calls, hardly needing to pay attention to the cardiologist. Hell, if he had done his job Jacob wouldn't have been on Eight Main anyway, with the patient in the next room having a steak, medium rare and wondering why all the delay in getting the salad dressing he had asked for. The attendings were on their own as they watched the straight line on the EKG. They knew that the resident on the bed, thumping on the chest of the chairman of the department of radiation therapy, was probably fracturing a few more ribs. But it didn't matter at that point. Nothing did. One of the nurses kept announcing, "I'm not getting a pressure."

"Jesus Christ, how the hell did this happen?"

The answer was supplied by a chorus of their peers. Jacob was a patient who should have been treated like other patients. They're told when they're ready to leave ICU. They don't announce it themselves. You don't transfer a guy who's been banged up in a car accident, bad enough to fracture a couple of ribs, to a goddam VIP floor. Not when he's got a history of an MI that's left him with a 30% reduction of cardiac function.

Suddenly everybody's talking about Jacob as just another patient. The "guy" who had this and should have had that. By then it was too late.

Just like that it was over. Enough department heads had made it to the floor so that they could have had an executive committee meeting. Jacob was there too. He was covered up then and put on the morgue stretcher, a metal one without a pad. Then they took him away. Father, husband, human being in his late fifties, who had saved so many others in their eighties, was gone.

The patient in the next room eventually got his salad dressing. By then he had lost his appetite and wrote a critical letter to the hospital's CEO, naming names. He received a reply, an apology, thanking him for the feedback.

CAUSATION

If that view from Eight Main was to die for, it wasn't the only one in sight. At least that was the opinion of Frederick Kosinski. Kosinski was a Hungarian refugee who had sought political asylum in America and had found economic paradise. The vista he associated with death was the one from his mansion on prestigious Star Island, the estate he shared with his brother Peter. Their home faced Government Cut, the man-made channel connecting the ocean off Miami Beach to the port of Miami. How many passengers, standing on the decks of cruise ships, had wished for the life of whoever resided within those stately walls?

I had met Frederick's brother first. He had scheduled an appointment in order for me to review the CAT scans of Frederick's brain. The films showed two distinct areas of tumor. Frederick's lung cancer had gone calling at the highest levels. Peter had been dispatched to canvass Dade County's neurologists and neurosurgeons about what could be done. His role as messenger seemed naturally cast. He sat forward in his chair with his legs together and his arms cradling Frederick's films in his lap as if he were holding a grandchild. But the only family left were he and Frederick. The string with which he had wrapped the Xray jackets labeled with Frederick's name belied the fortune those two had accumulated since emigrating to America thirty years before. Peter's hair and eyebrows were gray, and the tops of his ears lay buried under white tufts that spoke of a disregard for barbers. The loose folds of skin beneath his eyes sagged with a kind of gentleness. His lips were thin and had what seemed to be a natural upturn at either end. The sum total of his expression was one of understanding. It was as if he knew his mission was not so much in the result — that was inevitable — but solely in the effort. He was doing this for Frederick because that was what had been asked of him. I listened to the history as he read from a spiral notepad that he had removed from the inside of his jacket. The dates of the onset of symptoms, biopsies performed, and the kinds of medications and treatments which Frederick had received were recited with dispassionate clarity. How many times, in how many different doctors' offices, had he been through this routine? If the truth were known, he would have chosen a different path, returned to the old country with his afflicted brother to seek out one of the women who had been pointed out to them in their childhood as familiar with dybbuks. That's what it was going to take, the supernatural, if Frederick were going to survive. Peter listened to my opinion as if he had heard it all before, which I knew he had. I watched him retie those manila folders together and understood the ritual of his effort. It was how he managed what he had been asked to do, by tending to those films as if they were wares on an endless journey through villages he had once known. It wasn't to turn a profit, but to barter for peace of mind that had kept him on his way.

He thanked me and left the office as if he had no home. But several days later, a colleague provided me with a different perspective. The story of the two brothers was spreading like

Frederick's cancer. The privacy they had once shared was sundered by their unfulfilled search for an impossible cure. No detail seemed more telling than the litigation that Frederick was alleged to have begun against the owners of the cruise lines whose ships sailed from the port of Miami. As I listened to the particulars, what had been two white spots imposed upon an image of the brain merged to become the specter of a man. Frederick was not some peddler in the old country. He was a power broker in the world of industry and commerce, awash in the luxuries of his success. And among these none was more visible than that Star Island mansion. From the windows of his gilded bedroom Frederick had watched those great cruise ships gliding outward bound to their ports of call. Their size imposed a stillness on the surroundings. Their ponderous momentum seemed to slow the cars that raced along the MacArthur Causeway. They were Magritte at the window, red and blue striped bows and white anchors cutting through views with proportions that made no sense.

From Frederick's station of informed disease, those ships had begun to mock him. As each disappeared at sea he imagined that he could still hear the sound of the engines and in that sound a faint but fatal taunt. That stately disinterest at the progressive wasting of his life insinuated in his mind a notion of causality. He believed that the diesel smoke from the massive stacks of those ships had corrupted his body. What else could have been responsible for his lung cancer? He had never smoked and had understood that more than money was needed to ensure good health. He had pursued exercise and diet as if they were two more business associates to be courted for long-term benefits.

All of that had gone for naught. The irony, he thought, was that the exclusive home he had shared with his brother had been the source of his doom. Now he was drawn to his windows and those ships and their passengers with a measure of fatal fascination. As he watched, he became more certain with each passing ship that the smoke drifted unquestionably in his direction, and though it was invisible within seconds, he was sure that its poisonous residues settled upon him. No amount of heavy drapes or sealed windows could keep its distinctive odor away. When he saw passengers at the railings, he imagined one of them, throwing a perverse kind of life preserver over the side. It never seemed to fall to the water below, but would instead drift along with the smoke and, unseen, alight around his neck, settle upon his chest. Voyage after voyage this had occurred, even as he had hosted events for charity. Enough of those misplaced rings were fixed about him so that they had begun to restrict his breathing. Now they sought to drag him down to the common deep. That's how he had contracted cancer and had become a dying man.

With that understanding came a plan. He decided to approach his incurable illness as if it were just another business deal that awaited his proven techniques. They had always seemed to work in the past. He and his brother had discovered what could profit a man, had found that credit leads to credit, that the special favors intended for others as published in the Federal Register could be turned to their advantage as well. The two brothers, who had themselves been imported to their new country, became importers of goods. At first it was cloth, then manufactured shirts, and finally electronic components. It wasn't in the end what the commodity was so much as the commerce that defined its transfer. That's why he would have more to say about this dying thing. He wasn't going to let his life be taken away without a counterproposal, without making some of the bastards pay. First he dispatched his brother, Xrays in hand, to the appropriate specialists in Dade County, those he felt might be worth their salt by reputation or referral. He would lick this thing. He thought about the smugness of that victory in the pace of his breathing. He hadn't made it to that haughty window with its view of the passing ships without being able to deal with several issues at once. He'd get the bastards who had made him change course, diverted him from his financial affairs to a ceaseless preoccupation with his own breathing.

Not only was he going to survive, but there was money to be made as well. He would sue the sons of bitches who owned those ships, prove his theory that it was their diesel fumes that had caused his cancer. Before it was all over he'd end up owning the goddam cruise lines. His attorneys were on retainer, in house, as they say. He didn't ask for their opinion, he just told them what the hell he wanted done. They were instructed to file suit in U.S. District Court for the Southern District of Florida, alleging negligence and reckless endangerment on the part of the defendants. Each was named as the proximate cause of the plaintiff's lung cancer, and further stipulated in the bill of particulars as causing said condition in the plaintiff by knowingly violating clean air standards as specified in regulations published in the Federal Register. Additionally set forth were contentions that the plaintiff had never smoked or used tobacco products of any kind; that plaintiff had no known or reasonable cause of exposure to carcinogenic agents other than those discharged into the atmosphere by the defendants and their agents in the operation of cruise ships documented in service between the port of Miami and numerous Caribbean destinations; and that the defendants knew or should have known that their wanton acts of negligence exposed those residents, whose homes were located adjacent to the MacArthur Causeway,

Miami Beach, Florida, to significant risk of airborne respiratory illnesses, including, but not limited to, carcinoma of the lungs. He reread the copy of the notice delivered to him by the attorneys as if the words formed a liturgy upon which his salvation rested.

He chose to ignore the likely timetable of his action as reported to him by the attorneys. It would be several years from the assignment of a docket number to any actual trial, and years as well for all the necessary depositions to be completed, the so-called expert testimony paid for, transcribed, and filed by both sides. There was no reason to suppose that the defendants were simply going to go belly-up, offer a settlement just to dispose of the matter. His attorneys cautioned him that the defendants were entitled to information regarding the particulars of his state of health, adding: "Discovery in this sort of case, regarding the actual medical condition of the plaintiff, is proper, of course."

Suddenly, the bullshit legalese which Frederick had paid his attorneys to visit upon his competitors and adversaries when it suited his purpose had begun to cut the other way. Only now he was paying for it. The lawyers hadn't mentioned that his brother showing up in medical offices all over the county had made his plight something less than a well-guarded secret. Among themselves counsel for both sides agreed that it was a matter unlikely to see the light of day, "a dead issue," they acknowledged, with appropriate legal solemnity. Not that they envisioned Frederick's interests disappearing entirely. There were anticipated duties as trustee for a very sizable estate. No doubt matters would be complicated and take years and considerable sums before all Frederick's holdings were sorted out. As for defendant's counsel, they would be occupied with defending cruise lines against a steady stream of suits from disappointed passengers. Their days would be filled with complaints about food poisoning and sprained ankles, and the occasional missed appendicitis by a ship's doctor.

Shortly after the papers had been filed, before any notices for the taking of depositions could be served, Frederick developed his unremitting pain. It was resistant to pills and shots and round-the-clock nurses. No good to send his brother then. That's when I met Frederick, having almost forgotten Peter who had served as emissary. If there had ever been a resemblance between the two, the cancer had taken it away. Frederick had become a man drowning in himself. His eyes were sunken from lack of sleep and worse. To look at him was to be drawn into his dying — everything inward, sight, breath, fat, and muscle so that his loose and yellowed skin seemed borrowed from some other man. He was not the business magnate whose successful strategies had kept him afloat. There was no talk of blame or suits or what the smoke from some ships had done to him when I first met him in his room on Eight Main. It was simple then. All I had to do was stop the pain. And I did. Fixed it so that the nurses gave him morphine into a plastic reservoir underneath his scalp. From there the drug dissipated into his brain, into the water cavities, mixed as effectively as if churned by great propellers beneath the surface.

When Frederick went home from the hospital he was too invalid to stand. He asked to have pillows placed behind him and directed his nurse to open the windows wide. He wanted to breathe the fresh salt air. It was one of the reasons he had loved his house so much in the beginning. Just then a cruise ship passed by, its white smoke billowing from a blue and red painted stack. The contrast of those colors against the sky and sun filled him with a sense of wonder, and then he was standing upon the deck of that last ship as it departed from his view.

PREMONITION

To me, Frederick on that ship was the writer being ferried to the mountain's summit in Hemingway's "The Snows of Kilimanjaro." That's why I am always drawn from the morgue to the top of Judith's pavilion with its view of Mount Sinai. It is the progress of my own premonitory pilgrimage, what Steve had termed the declension of life. We pass, he had once said, from knowing that we are going to die, to understanding who we are, and at the end may perceive we are dying.

That I was going to die overcame me at five. It was 1949, and the boy that I had been waited inside the house of his friend, his could-be twin, listening to the sounds of a family in their kitchen. The voices of the parents rose above the bells of silverware and the whistle of brewing tea. Sunlight streamed through the windows of an indoor porch where the boy waited. He became distracted by that light. It pointed him to a wooden toy chest that fit perfectly under a white windowsill. He had rummaged through that box many times. As collections were to five-year-olds, it never seemed to give up the same object, might just as well have been bottomless.

His eyes fell upon a cornet, more toy than instrument, that lay in an opened velvet case. A green-stained cloth muted the flared bell. A silvered mouthpiece was stoppered in place. The sun reflected from that horn like a signal upon some vast plane. Like a boy who trekked alone, he was drawn to it. He reached past a baseball glove and a puzzle board to grasp the pearl-topped pistons and pull it free.

There are songs to this life whose source we may never know, that reach us as if in a dream. And so he heard at that moment a far-off tune that played within his mind. It might just as well have been a dirge. That cornet was the Excaliber of his youth and he was kinged by the court of mortality. For at that instant he knew that he should one day die. If he shivered with the loneliness of that discovery, perhaps it was death slipping by, off to some other call, a task now done. Despite the summer sun, the moment froze like an image on an ice-covered pond. He was a five-year-old boy on a Saturday morning, waiting for his friend, and he had been robbed of his endless future. And why? Why that morning, on that sunlit porch, as he held that neglected horn? Nothing had changed, no clouds blocked the morning light, no shadows cast a pall upon the paraphernalia of youth. There were no cries from the next room or from afar. But this he knew, that something or someone had called to him; and it had done so through that horn like a trumpet from on high.

I kept the memory of that dark and magical instrument secret for forty years, less from a fear of disbelief than of awful fulfillment. It was a mystery that seemed more impenetrable with each passing year, until its solution and sharing were fittingly brought about by my wife. We had found ourselves in a used bookstore in a far-off room with ceiling-high stacks and piles of uncatalogued volumes on the floor. She had handed me a book of photographs, a remembered collection from her own childhood, had commended it to me as one of her favorites. Since what was hers I wished to be ours, I was bound to its contents. It contained the editor's choice of the more memorable photographs first published in *Life* magazine. I turned the pages and reviewed my youth, the forties and fifties frozen in their time. I saw him then, and knew that I had seen him before. He was in a photograph in a book my parents had kept in the recessed shelf of their Art Deco nightstand. The black rotary phone with its circular label, Blackburn 8-7723, may have even rested upon it from time to time.

The photograph was of Chief Petty Officer Graham Jackson, a navy musician, playing his accordion the day after President Roosevelt had died as the body was being carried to a train. It depicted Jackson in uniform, his dress cap and face raised toward God Almighty. His black face was streaked with tears, his eyes and lips cried the cry of the mourning. He had not stopped playing. His accordion was the armour at his chest. Its white and black horizontal keys climbed the stairway to his grief. The caption revealed "Goin' Home," to be his song of tribute. To either side and slightly out of focus were the bereaved and the curious. To see that photograph was to hear the death knell of a fallen leader.

"Why is that man crying?" the boy would have asked his mother.

"President Roosevelt had died, honey. Everybody cried."

Forty years later, surrounded by books and in the available light of a fall afternoon, Jackson's accordion gave reason to that fatal cornet. In the Saturday morning of my youth the horn that the boy held had returned him unseen to that photograph. Jackson's tears were for me, the boy, the father of the man. If he hadn't died yet, he one day would. If the far-off tune were

"Goin' Home," so much the better. The first declension had been completed. The second, *Who am I,* was still decades in the making.

The discovered origin of that Saturday morning revelation gave purpose to a second and only slightly later event. Once again it occurred while the boy waited on that magical sun porch. This time he was suited up, cowboy for the great outdoors. He had learned not to devote his idle time to that foreboding chest of toys. The grandfather's clock that stood in the foyer of his friend's house held no similar prohibition. The boy reached out and lassoed with his waxed and braided rope the key to that clock. It had been waiting for him, innocently inserted into the beveled glass door behind which the pendulum of time announced its purpose. He cinched the knot around that precarious key. At first it reacted like a lure. Gave a slight feint as if to say, "I'm ready." His practiced skill on that remembered morning, a herd of cattle just outside, was not yet fully proven. As he pulled, the key resisted out of all proportion, stubbornly holding on to its simple task. The question that I posed, four decades later, was why did that boy persist? Did he have the intent of changing time? Perhaps it was his boyhood version of Frederick's resolve. He would turn those ornate hands back two months and stop that watching clock just before the light from a cornet had caught his eye. Farfetched, I thought from forty years. More likely a boy's bravado pure and simple. There was no far-off tune that day, just the exhilaration of the thing caught and a purpose to be fulfilled. By the time his friend had obediently finished his breakfast, the struggle was under way.

"Help me wrestle this key," the boy called out. Room enough for two at the end of that rope. Together they could bring in the last calf strayed from the herd just this side of El

Paso. Not much of a match really, determined cowboys against a key that could barely flash its intent. How much strength do two five-year-olds have? The key moved again. It seemed as if it were about to surrender to their leaning determination. Then, from my adult perspective, something or someone decided to change the game. It thought that maybe two five-year-olds didn't add up to ten. Certainly not with one of them already knowing better. Hadn't he held that cornet only two months before? And so with a pendular momentum, either pushed or pulled, the clock pitched forward.

The wonder of it all, both sets of parents would later, much later, agree, was that it missed both boys, seeing how close they had been in that after-breakfast time of their inseparable youths. Instead the clock had simply knelled its regret. But the rope had left a trail of explanation and a fuse for the jeweler-father of the boy's friend.

"That grandfather clock has been in our family since Christian Bixler opened the first jewelry store in America," he kept repeating.

"Keeping time for all these years."

The clock was repaired and returned to its former station, cabinetwork really. It stayed in that house with my friend's family until his sister fell backward off the front porch. His parents decided to move to the country then. They set the clock in their living room. It faced a wide picture window that for some reason was unseen by birds in full flight. Their journey's end would be announced with a random thud. Their eyeless heads and faded feathers would gather on an outside porch until my friend's father would collect them in a dustpan and throw them just beyond the mowed grass.

I don't know where that clock is now, keeper of American time, "in the family for almost two hundred years." It had sat in the sunlight on a Saturday morning and kept time with the sounds of a family at breakfast. It had watched a boy in a sunroom who saw that his life would end, watched him lay a cornet back in a wooden toy chest, even though it was already too late.

As for that far-off tune, the boy had kept it to himself. Although he thought he might have heard it a few years later as he and his sister sat on the stairs in a Philadelphia row house, not unlike the one that Ivan had visited. There wasn't anyone skewered to the banister. Instead, the boy's uncle, his father's brother, had died. It was after the funeral, family and friends gathered at the house of the deceased for a postmortem buffet. As the boy sat on those stairs balancing a paper plate on his lap, his cousin, whose father had died, spoke about classmates and about school. He didn't seem to notice the abyss that had opened up between himself and his father. The boy knew it was too wide to stretch a rope across to try to pull the lost father back.

PRECEDENCE

The boy had been banished from the Garden, tasted the bittersweet fruit of mortality. He was going to die and over the years his own father and grandfather would show him how. His grandfather died at eighty. At least that was his calculated age. The exact date of his birth was unknown. He had chosen July 4th, contending that he remembered hearing loud noises at the time. He had adopted the country's birthday as a teenager, shortly after arriving in Philadelphia, emigrating from Eastern Europe by way of Montreal. It was quiet, though, when he died, a warm June day. At his funeral, the hearse followed a meandering road to the grave site, something about one last time past his territory. The route bordered the forks of the Delaware, Easton in eastern Pennsylvania. Had he continued south that day he most likely would have stopped in Upper Black Eddy, among the Pennsylvania Dutch. He had often spoken of how they would insist, "Mr. Rosenthal, if you don't come in for lunch, we'll never forgive you." That was when he was a traveling salesman, buying and selling old gold, termed estate jewelry now. He had weights and a scale and some hydrochloric acid in a brown bottle to make sure he wasn't buying fool's metal. He had done that on either side of being a furniture salesman. Throwing in a lamp with the end tables was his secret to closing a sale. He was responsible for more bedroom suites between Easton and Stroudsberg than his nearest competitor, Benny Phillips. Their field of battle was the showroom floor of Louis M. Ralph and Sons. Each day they took up their positions at the far left, just in front of the partitioned office reserved for management. No one entered that store without their taking notice. Even as a visiting grandson the boy was never deprived of a greeting that seemed just one step away from being shown a dining room set. Bona fide customers would either walk straight to those watchful servants or begin to meander. If they made it to the living room section they were Benny's, dining or bedroom suites, Pop's. There was also the glorious possibility that in response to the opening prayer, "May I help you?" these newly arrived members of the congregation would respond with an answer that seemed to emanate from on high, Yom Tov prayers answered in spades, "Yes, I'd like to see Mr. Rosenthal. He sold us our last bedroom set twenty years ago." Or, in the unknowable ways of the Almighty, "Mr. Phillips, please." It was the return of a satisfied customer to the prodigal sons. Whoever was not mentioned would fade back into the office, no doubt to check on deliveries or some other aspect of service from which those sons of bitches who had made the fateful wrong choice would now be deprived. It was a daily struggle that dragged on for what seemed like longer than the Punic wars. Despite their ceaseless competition, protocol dictated that each time the boy visited the store he was required to shake hands and say hello to Mr. Phillips. He would get his head rubbed then and an ear pulled. It was a rite of identification which may have also conferred battlefield immunity in that no man's land of potential customers.

I can't remember now who won the ultimate battle, if Benny was there on that June afternoon. At the graveside I shook hands with my grandfather's doctor, Joe Brau. He was the physician who had seen him through his cancer of the kidney, cured at seventy; a first stroke at seventy-five from which he recovered, and the final one, five years later, that had left him paralyzed on his right side and unable to speak. "Not a livable life," as Dr. Scott would later say. I had already been taught that lesson. My grandfather had developed a complication following his stroke. A blockage in his iliac artery had cut off the circulation to his leg. It was his left, the one that he could still move. The option of amputation was raised with the family, which in this case started with my mother. She had stayed at his bedside every day during his six-week hospitalization. It was a death watch for the father who had taken her by the hand to New York, told the agent, "Let me show you how my little girl can sing and dance." That's how she had broken into vaudeville at fifteen, left high school, not to return to formal academia until she was elected president of the women's auxiliary at Lafayette College in my freshmen year. She had matriculated to the boulevard of dreams and the bright lights of an adolescent career. It was what fed her parents and sisters and paid their rent during the Depression.

The curriculum had instructed her that she was only as good as her last performance. The applause always died down. She learned never to get off the stage, but stay right up there where she knew her stuff. In the hospital as her father lay dying, it was she who held his hand as she sat by his bedside and watched the stage door father who had lived with us for the five years between his two strokes. It fell on her shoulders, along with her two sisters, to decide whether to operate or to let him go. Not to operate but to let the gangrenous leg take the rest of his body, like Edith Small's foot had wanted to do, was the decision. To be wheelchair-bound, unable to speak or understand what was being said, was not what they wished for him. They projected upon his ineloquent form a desire not to exist in such an altered state, a preference of death to amputated invalidism. The decision to let him go was not second-guessed. In the end, except for his rapid breathing, as if he were struggling to catch up, he seemed not to be in pain. Maybe that's why I thanked Joe Brau. He had kept my grandfather sedated, given him enough morphine so that perhaps despite his loss of speech his dreams were still conversant. I think of my grandfather when I see a patient of a similar age in the emergency room, a wife or daughter by the side of the stretcher. As I approach them to explain that the CAT scan shows more blood than brain where the left hemisphere should be, I see Joe Brau talking to my mother again and my grandfather on the open road to Upper Black Eddy.

If my grandfather was taken by the hand to death, one final audition, my father reached out to shake its hand. There was no question about his age, authentic, as old as the century when he died in 1980. He had been my mother's lawyer from Yale, the one she had set her sights on after coming back home from vaudeville. He practiced at the bar in Northampton County for fifty years. Loved the law, as he used to say, and was always his own man. He should have been a writer. No one understood clients and the entanglements of their lives as well as he. He listened to their stories of strife and disagreements with ecclesiatical patience. When he counseled them he could be authoritative and ingratiating at the same time. I would hear him on the phone and know to whom he was speaking by the dialect he had assumed. Once while talking to someone named Bubba, he adopted a southern drawl to his advice, as if they were both on the front porch of a general store, sharecroppers leading a hard life. He had an Asian business associate in a start-up cable TV venture. When they conversed my father's eyes would narrow and his sentences pidginize as he reviewed their options like a waiter repeating the specials from column B.

"You can't con a con man," was one of his sayings and if a client thought he could there would be the obligatory dressing-down. It was the legal profession's version of boot camp, the client brayed at until the message was clear who was counsel and who needed help.

This attorney at law was as much Damon Runyon as Felix Frankfurter. The track was his other world. An afternoon at the flats followed by a twilight session at the trotters was the equivalent of a thirty-six hole extravaganza to a committed golfer. He loved everything about the races. From valet parking to the last losing tickets abandoned at his feet, he immersed himself in the event. He was surrounded by many of his former and current clients, all equalized in their pursuit of a handicapper's advantage. He cried at movies and once in the late thirties had promised a local magistrate who thought the Nazis weren't all that bad, that before they arrived on American shores, "I'll get you first."

He wrote poems to my mother when my sister and I were born. Anecdotes of his courthouse appearances are still recounted by those with whom he practiced. At the dinner honoring him for fifty years at the bar, he spoke about awakening from anesthesia after undergoing surgery for an abdominal aneurysm that couldn't be repaired. He had asked that the TV be turned on, hoping to catch the results from Aqueduct. Instead what he said he had seen were the faces of the four sitting judges, thought he hadn't made it through the surgery. He spoke about his illness and added that if he didn't live much longer he'd make out all right. It was four years later, an additional four years with my sister's three children growing up with a grandfather, that he was taken to the emergency room. The abdominal aneurysm had ruptured. The surgeon on call explained the dire nature of his condition. Unless surgery could be done, he would most certainly die.

My mother and sister were with him and described him later as more than lucid. He seemed from their descriptions to have imposed a measured perspective on what was happening. I don't know if he spoke to that Indian surgeon with a hint of British servitude. The answer was no. No surgery. It was time to get on with other things. They took him to the intensive care unit. He died before I could get there from Asheville, North Carolina, where we had been vacationing. My *Look Homeward, Angel* flight was too late.

Whenever I think of that day and my father's death, I hear him speaking to me. "This is how it's done."

VISION

The deaths of my father and grandfather awakened within me the five-year-old boy who I had been, the boy who had heard the lost note. And since Chris Harlan he has not been alone. Chris, too, discovered the worm at his core. But his enlightenment was more dire. At age eight Chris's freedom should have been inviolable, defined as it was by his skateboard. He could ride it almost anywhere and anytime. It was like skiing, but he didn't need money or have to get on a plane, which is what he and his mother would have had to do, living as they did in Fort Lauderdale. His mother couldn't have afforded that anyway, not since his father had left. But she had found a job and if she wasn't home right after school, she was there soon enough. By the time he was finished playing and had done his homework she would come through the door and get right to making dinner, usually pasta and a vegetable. Once a week they would have hamburger, his favorite.

Chris's afternoons passed quickly on that skateboard. It was his all-weather American flyer. He was good on it too. Not to the point of doing flips or testing ramps like he had seen on TV, he didn't need to do that. He was content to simply navigate the sidewalks and parking lots in his neighborhood. He had his own private paths to wherever he wished to go, even to Indiana where his father lived, where he went each year over Christmas vacation. His mother would put him on the plane and a stewardess would pamper him during the flight. Once they moved him to first class. His father would be waiting when the plane landed in Indianapolis. Then they would drive eighty miles to the small town where his father's new family lived. It was just the two of them, his dad arranged it that way. Sometimes when he looked out the window of that car, it was like being on his skateboard. The other cars seemed to be in slow motion, even if they were passing his father. The rest of life too, all of it seemed to be at a different speed. That's the way it was on his board. Cars, people on the sidewalk, other kids, all of them seemed to be in another world, as if worlds were defined by speed and motion and he had found his own special and private one.

That was why he was so content playing alone and why he had made it his secret. He thought if he told his mother or best friend, his world might go away. Same board, same sidewalks and parking lots, but the secret once revealed, denied. He feared that some barrier might appear and prevent him from breaking into his private pace of life that he found so safe.

It was just that world of motion, made personal, that gave him such an extraordinary view of his accident. Silly, a navigator of his experience and expertise, losing it on a curve. Better he was alone. His friends would have simply laughed. His carelessness seemed to come out of nowhere. Or perhaps one of the other worlds had thrown his timing off. But for whatever reason his momentum and his skateboard were suddenly separate. And he knew it was coming. No way to stop it really. Even with the first notion of, "Here I go," he wasn't concerned. His arms and legs had always followed his exact commands. He had stopped wearing elbow pads and wrist guards almost a year before. When he did fall, it seemed natural for him to land on his hip or shoulder and roll out of it like a paratrooper he had seen in a movie on the last night of his visit with his dad, just the two of them again. This fall was as he expected. He saw the pavement and felt his hands and wrists tuck neatly to his chest. Maybe this would be the one he'd come right out of, right back up on the board and continue on, like he had planned it that way. He got to thinking about just how he might do that. He never really saw the stick, more like a branch. It had been placed in the short Florida grass by a conscientious retiree who had noticed it on the sidewalk while coming out of the post office. It was a yard long, with progressively smaller twigs at one end that seemed like a hand.

Things probably wouldn't have turned out as badly if that were the end that had caught his face. The hand might have just scratched him, so that when his mother came home she would have asked, "How in the world?" not thinking which world. As if she wouldn't have known he had been skateboarding. Each night during his pre-bed, post-bath inspection she had inquired as to every scratch and bruise that had come his way. But it wasn't the end of the branch with a hand made out of twigs that awaited him. It was the other end, that had been broken by a truck as it backed out of the post office parking lot. The driver had seen it in his sideview mirror, assumed it would simply snap. But that branch had not gone easily. It had held on by bark and fiber until an outer breaking had occurred and then didn't give up entirely until the mirror was snagged or perhaps grasped by that hand. Then at last the separation was complete.

As Chris fell he saw the tree and the sunlight through its leaves with one eye. He had by reflex closed his other eye, the down-side. What happened next didn't feel all that bad. Not that he didn't know something was wrong. There was a sensation. It wasn't what might be called a blinding pain. His cornea had been spared. Millions of years of sensory evolution, focused upon the surface of his eye, had remained untested. Instead, it was the skin of his eyelid just beyond the corner of his eye that was violated, penetrated by a sliver of wood, part of a branch, that only an hour before was inherent to a tree. His orbit was startled by the intrusion, unthinkably close to his globe, another world unto itself. As if guided by design, that would-be arrow, propelled by the weight of his head, became embedded in the base of his skull behind the eye, in an almost secret nook, wood in a place reserved for nerves that directed the movement of his eye, and the blood that was draining from it.

If only in Chris's world of motion he could have remained perfectly still then, lain there until his mother got off the bus and passed by on her way home. If anyone asked, "Hey kid are you OK?" he could have simply answered, "Yes." When his mother found him, she could have called an ambulance. Its crew might have known enough to move him *en bloc* like a sculpture in the Museum of Modern Art that had broken new ground for its relationship of life forms, the boy with a branch growing out of his eye. They could have laid him on his side in the back of the ambulance, enough room for the branch once the oxygen tanks had been moved. His head could have been cradled in hands like his father's until they reached the hospital. A nurse and doctor would have come outside and decided not to move him until the neurosurgeon and ophthalmologist arrived. They would have climbed into the ambulance, ducking under the intravenous lines as if those lines were police tape at a crime scene. Hospital security would have been called to keep the media back, preventing the technician with a minicam from Channel Four from being caught by a hand of twigs. His mother would have stayed by his side until the firemen arrived with a chain saw. The neurosurgeon, hoping his career or worse was not about to be ended, would have held the branch on either side of the planned cut. Chris would have felt the hand of the ophthalmologist pressed against his cheek and sensed a collective relief as he was partially pruned from that branch. They would have taken him then on a stretcher, still on his side with a pillow under his head, the smell of the hospital sheets making up for what he couldn't see while he kept both eyes closed as they had asked him to do. His mother would have walked by his side, holding his hand. There wouldn't have been much pain. After a while, after they had finished their Xrays and scans, there would have been the nothingness of anesthesia. Five and a half hours later, what would have passed instantly to him, he would have awakened in the recovery room, both eyes patched. Famous in the hospital as the boy who had been brought to the emergency room with a branch growing out of his eye.

All that of course, had he remained perfectly still. But the momentum of his fall, which had been sufficient to cause a sliver of that broken branch to penetrate through his orbit and to become embedded in the base of his skull, had carried his face and head past that fateful meeting. Not so far as to produce a spinal injury and paralysis, "Thanks to God," as the Cuban woman who worked with his mother would later say. But far enough to break that branch a second time. Only a splinter of wood was left behind.

In Chris's world this was seen only by his horrified orbit, aghast at the near destruction of his globe and by the equally outrageous comings and goings so implausibly unannounced. And then all was still. He didn't have to be careful. The branch lay at his side, as remote as a branch should be from the eye of a child at play. Impossibly, he was still able to see. Although his vision was blurred out of that eye, as if the thing seen resides inside, and vision simply leaves. He reached up and felt his face and the corner of the eye. There was blood, but not as much as when his friend had hoisted a cut log into a tree, a crude, guillotine-like affair. It had dropped almost a foot before it grazed Chris's scalp. His friend's mother had driven him to the emergency room, but the bleeding had stopped and he didn't need stitches. In his childhood innocence he had mistaken what had happened for an accident. He thought that maybe this bleeding would stop too. If his mother noticed something, he'd tell her what she would already know, "Skateboarding."

It was getting dark, a little earlier it seemed than the day before. He decided to go home and wait for his mother, maybe even surprise her and make them both some cheese sandwiches. He was feeling sad for her, as if his having fallen would be one more problem she didn't need, not with all that she had on her mind. He walked home in the normal world. A boy he didn't know rode by on a bicycle and two ladies looked at him as they passed by on the sidewalk. He carried his skateboard as if it were a book bag and he had no idea what it was for. By the time he arrived home, it was darker still. He felt his stomach tightening. He wasn't hungry any longer, couldn't face the kitchen or the thought of bread and cheese. He decided to wait for his mother on the couch.

He was sleeping when she came through the door, unusual for him, and so she went right to his side, more for a wake-up kiss than anything else. Seeing his face raised a feeling in her that she didn't have time to understand. She gripped his shoulder as much to steady herself as to awaken him.

"Chris is everything all right? What happened to your eye?"

Immediately his right eye, the good one, opened and he looked at her. There was a sense of relief that seemed to come from that eye, his vision touching her.

"I guess I hit it when I fell skateboarding this afternoon, Mom. It doesn't hurt too much and I could still see when I got home. What's for dinner?"

She had turned on the end table light, turned it all three clicks so she could get a better look. A real shiner, he'd had one of those before, she remembered — just like his dad. There was something else, what could have been dried tears, except tears didn't dry brown. There was rust on his face like he was the Tin Man in the *Wizard of Oz*. Where the tears, or whatever they were, had started there was a darkened and bruised area. She thought he might have been bitten by a spider. He let her touch it, it wasn't that tender, but she felt the rough edges of dried blood that had sealed the wound. Even if she had tried, the swelling around his eye would have prevented her from lifting his lid. He smiled at her, but there was something about those tears. They robbed her of the reassurance from his smile, made her worry about how much money they'd want at the emergency room. She and Chris weren't covered by insurance at the motel where she had found a job.

On the way to the hospital in their neighbor's car, Chris noticed only one world of motion. The first Xrays explained what his mother had thought was perhaps an insect bite. There was air underneath the skin next to his eye. The bite was a cut. Something had penetrated into his orbit, the doctor explained, although it didn't seem to have left anything behind. He had ordered a CAT scan to make sure. The eye was still intact. With a nurse holding Chris's head and his mother both of his arms, the doctor managed to open his eyelid. Although they seemed blurred, Chris could count two fingers. The doctor said it was a good sign, and more, adding that usually with air in the orbit, the globe has been disrupted and vision lost. He was a lucky boy. What Chris was thinking about, almost mourning, was the loss of his other world. Twice now it hadn't been there, when he walked home after his fall and on the way to the hospital. Whether it was the doctor prying open his eyelid or something else, he was in pain now. It wasn't just his eye. His whole head hurt. They admitted him after the CAT scan. "Overnight observation," suggested the Broward County neurosurgeon who had been called. The ophthalmologist thought it was a good idea too — even though the globe wasn't disrupted, he wasn't sure about the muscles that moved the eye. He'd have to wait for the swelling to go down to see if they were affected. Even so, that could be corrected with an operation.

"Home in a day or two," said the neurosurgeon as he tousled Chris's hair. "Back on that skateboard."

Who knows when the self leaves? By the next morning Chris's mother had noticed he was different. Why wouldn't he be? He had a fever and was in pain. If he showed no interest in what she was saying it was just his child's way of getting through. But it was more than that. His brain had already taken seed. The wood that was left behind from that branch, that had remained undetected by the CAT scan, was beginning to sprout. No shoots or buds were destined in that unlikely hiding place. Instead the growing things were bacteria, dispersed by the blood that bathed that branch, innumerable in their want. Caught by the nearby brain, they settled in, sacrificed to the antibiotics what was their due, but otherwise prospered. It was a place dark and warm with endless food. Chris's thoughts became a tissue culture, and one by one were subverted to the greater need.

It would be a week, and three more CAT scans, before the doctors were sure he had a brain abscess. He was taken to surgery, had it removed, came back almost the way he had been before his mother had let go of his hand. His father was there. Chris didn't remember him right away. Didn't seem to know about Indiana or those rides that just the two of them had shared from the airport, home.

Chris never rode his skateboard again. In all he had four operations, the last one to remove the wood his surgeons knew had to be there but just couldn't find. Three years later, enough time for the responsibility of his lost world to be attributed to his doctors, he limped to the witness stand. Watching him, it looked as if he moved in his own pace and time. As he dragged his leg, with one arm perpetually held to his chest, it seemed as if he were forever falling.

VULNERABILITY

In the end it didn't seem important that Chris's vision had been preserved, not in comparison to what he had irretrievably lost. His gaze out of either eye could settle on nothing familiar. It didn't matter then what he was seeing, the sight of a tree or a fallen branch held no particular warning. This was not so with the boy that I had been, who had chosen to become a neurosurgeon. In my last year of medical school during a four-month rotation at the Cleveland Clinic, I discovered the limits of our gaze.

As a prelude to my neurosurgical residency, I had elected to round each day at six and six with the clinic's neurosurgical residents. The exposure to clinical problems was endless. I saw patients with tumors and spinal abnormalities, and those with unremitting pain. The full range of my future specialty seemed represented with only the exception of trauma. For that the residents rotated through Metro General. So exactly how the patient we had come upon had been admitted to the clinic was somewhat a mystery, atypical for the usual rounding fare. We had entered his room and the presenting resident began the history. As he spoke he was positioned between me and the patient. The bandage he had begun to unravel seemed to be nothing more than a usual head dressing, four-inch white gauze, wrapped from behind the ears to the forehead. It was the final coronation for all who emerged from the operating room after undergoing a craniotomy. But as the resident stepped back I saw no incison line across the scalp with stitching reminiscent of a baseball. Instead the face of a Negro boy appeared, but in sections, as if inviting segregated contemplation. To the lower right were the normal visual cues of a young black male, full lips, a prominent cheek and a sharp jaw. But the upper left did not continue that start, and I had no experience to absorb the sight. For whose sight was I thinking about at that moment, mine or his? Where his left eye should have been, in its hallowed sanctuary, its lid and eyelashes in gentle landscape, the brow projecting against unexpected assault, there was instead palpable Picasso. The canvas was three-dimensional with fluids not yet dry, and all vision lost. As I looked, the distinction between the boy and myself vanished. A darkness from that blinded eye was cast upon me. When I reached to feel my face intact, a sensible contour, gentle resistance, a world of globe to serve in definition, there was confusion about what or whom I was touching. The boy or myself? A wound? Some independent object from another time and place? When I tried to turn away, avert my gaze, what moved? Which head? Whose eye? If he cried would the tears burn? And when that eye moved as he took a breath, something was terribly wrong. At last there was nothing for me to hold on to and no sense in crying out, "This is not supposed to be." Instead I heard a voice of self-protection, "It's not safe to have everything shut down while you are in a standing position, sir." The source of that warning was right. One might incur an injury that in its bandaged naiveté could reveal a profession-threatening vulnerability. Needs to confine himself to research. Can't really deal with patients down in the trenches. I backed away from the bedside, hearing only part of what was being said about a planned exenteration, that euphemism for plucking out. Unless that was done, the decaying remnants of what had once been an eye would begin to signal the immune system. That would provoke a response which would threaten the good eye, its anonymity lost in the agonal dissolution of its former mate. Any pleadings that a terrible mistake was being made, that the boy was being placed in even more jeopardy by this bureaucratic stupidity, would be to no avail. There is no source of reason or anthropomorphic mercy at the cellular level. In the end, a withered pit where once had been an eye.

I sat down on a conveniently placed chair opposite the bed, the one in which a friend or family member might sit and stare, talk for a little while until it was time to go. Having made it to that chair, I felt somewhat safer. There was less distance to fall, perhaps less humiliation when I awoke. I placed my head between my knees in sheepish confession. This was something too much for me. If there were a doctor present who could help this boy it would have to be someone else. I needed help myself.

My colleagues, whether through genuine concern or self-recognition, a recaptured memory of when they had needed to absent themselves, gathered around me like cops responding to an assist-officer call. For the moment the patient with half a face was forgotten. Whether it was the hands on my shoulder, or my head between my knees, all had returned to focus. Deep breaths dispelled a hint of nausea. Perhaps what I had experienced was simply a mistake, not enough sleep, or the home fries in the cafeteria that morning might have been just a little off.

The head dressing was reapplied, and the group, its excitement now passed, moved on down the hall and I with them, my legs working, composure restored and pride surprisingly intact. Maybe in a way I had been their surrogate for the horror. I may have dissipated for the others what lurked somewhere within them, a latent desire to reject what they were seeing. Instead of an outcast, I was still their comrade. The hope and promise of one day being like them, "Somebody here need a neurosurgeon?" not undone, but made more human in my definition.

Yet that episode could not be forgotten or simply relegated to anecdotal status. Even though there was no light-headedness when I subsequently saw the awful destruction of gunshot wounds or surveyed the damage that resulted when human bodies were hurled against asphalt or tree, I had the suspicion that eyes in a disrupted and vestigial state could cast a spell upon me. It was a prediction of vulnerability that was confirmed several years later as I stood across an operating table from Dr. Scott to assist in a "minor" case. The patient suffered as Nelson Graves had from tic douloureux. She was unable to brush her teeth, or take a sip a water, without experiencing what felt like a frog's tongue with a blade on the end brutishly flailing about her face. Her nerve endings never seemed prone to exhaustion or appeared likely to succumb to the kind of dullness that might envelope the victim of a beating. Dr. Scott had planned a straightforward surgical approach. He would find the infraorbital nerve beneath the skin of her cheek just below her right eye and destroy it. It would be white and glistening as it exited from the skull through a bony canal. Dr. Scott asked for a scalpel and incised the delicate skin along a line the patient herself might have traced with eyeliner a thousand times before.

There are wounds that seem to weep more than bleed, and this was one of them. The red crease opened by his blade produced hesitant drops of blood-like tears. I delayed the application of a sponge as much in respect for the appropriateness of those red tears as for the inconsequential effect they would have had upon the surgical field. They might as well have been dried and rusted for all the alarm they engendered. Dr. Scott adjusted the surgical drapes and opened the eyelid to confirm the exact location of the patient's pupil before embarking on deeper dissection. There it was again, an isolated eye, a surgical laceration with hardly any blood beneath it, and staring at what? Even though the patient was anaesthetized, there was a sense of vision out of that eye lighting upon me. I was back in medical school rounding at the Cleveland Clinic. I couldn't remember if I were in front of a mirror, looking at myself, my own eye, with perhaps some invisible speck insistent upon attention. And if that eye were mine, then the rest of me should have been under those drapes as well. It seemed best to lie down so as not to strain the connections between eye and self. Only this time I was surgically scrubbed and gowned. It would have been considered bad form to fall into that wound, although it seemed to be the place that was calling to me. I stepped back and cast my absentee ballot. No matter, the scrub nurse could fill in, "Here, hold this retractor."

At last there could be no mistake. Somewhere back in time, and perhaps as obscure as a forgotten photograph, I had been signed by a spurious eye. It had left me with a glaring exception to the protective detachment needed in my profession.

He came back to me then, the only dwarf I ever knew, in the circus that never left town. He was a photographer and his name was Mace Bugen. If he had been cast in a television show it could have been called "Bugen's Raiders." The opening credits would have portrayed him sweeping across the vista of hometown Easton in his UJA-emblazoned jeep. Instead of a rear-mounted machine gun and a flying scarf at the ready, it would have been a press camera, two-hander with a side-mounted flash that umbrellaed the sun and stopped in time whomever Mace chose to shoot.

When Mace stood on a chair that camera was his great equalizer. To look at the photographs of our day-camp baseball team or of the three buglers at morning reveille, future lawyer, industrialist, and neurosurgeon, there's no way to tell the photographer was only three-and-a-half-feet tall. What little legs he had, bent out like a cowboy's, no pony that small. In my mind's eye, Mace could have passed for almost normal if those legs could have been straightened out a bit. There was nothing to be done about his eyes. He had an element of exophthalmos, his eyes protruding past his aging face. They were wide-angled as well, reptilian in their independence. It seemed impossible to step beyond his field of vision. Whoever tried, as Mace beseeched those of us who were his equals to pose on command, would be summoned back by his mysterious voice. Its origin seemed not so much from his throat as from those eyes. It was ventriloquy made visual. His gaze always seemed fixed to mine just before the flash. And amidst the sound of that metallic sun, Mace became six feet tall.

Whether it was the magic of his camera or my fear of his deformities, I sought an accommodation. I would make him walk tall if he would record for me the life of the mind. Whatever maladies I beheld, I imagined Mace fixing them forever through the permanent gaze of his camera's lens. We started with him, everything but his eyes. I could picture his legs and the way he walked. It wasn't so much one foot in front of the other, as it was thigh to side. His hands had uniform digits, his thumbs equal in length to his index fingers, well-suited to that camera. He had almost no neck. His head seemed precariously balanced on his shoulders as if it might be gone after the next flash. But it was Mace on his chair that fixed in my mind's eye the images of those whom I would seek to heal. There was the big-headed boy I saw through a ballpark batting cage in the days before hydrocephalus was a treatable malady. When there was someone with a limp — *snap* — Mace would get them. "Have you walking straight, someday," would be my caption. My sister was reaching across a table, "Let me help with the tea, Mommy." Another one shows her in a prom dress with a chiffon shawl draped over her shoulders, hiding the scar on an otherwise perfect arm that cradles her corsage. A frail man and his failing wife were the parents of a friend. They died within six months of each other when my friend was eight and his brother six. The girl on the playground had a hearing aid that had become dislodged. The sound that I heard seemed part ambulance, part meltdown. But none of these remembered images are of eyes. Perhaps because I could never look at Mace's eyes without hearing his disarticulated voice. That was the voice that had engaged me at the Cleveland Clinic and later as I stood across the table from Dr. Scott. Mace's height and my profession had been made secure with but one exception.

I have learned to care for patients within this limitation. There hasn't been a third episode of such abrupt departure, not even with Maggie Hart. She was injured when a concrete block came through her windshield. It was as if someone had been dangling a chunk of highway debris on a string, delighting in the way it swung back and forth like a yo-yo, and then guiding it toward her car. It might have been the yo-yo man himself. I had seen him after school "walking the dog," outside of Hershey's ice cream store on fall afternoons. It was his job to travel from Maryland to Maine as the northeast regional representative for Duncan Yo-yo in the early fifties. That was before the suspicion of child molesters would have precluded such a profession. Maybe it was a bogus operation even then. It would have been a perfect cover at a time when the country believed that there were yo-yo companies which would actually dispatch a grown man, alone, out there except for his yo-yo, whose job it was to show kids how to "walk the dog" and "rock the baby" and keep "the cat in the cradle." He must have been authentic though. No one in a white apron with chocolate sauce on the front came outside to chase him away. There was a new display of Duncan Yo-yos on the counter by the register. Any of us who had seventy-five cents for the deluxe model that could glow in the dark, and were inspired by the possibilities of the yo-yo as masterfully demonstrated, could be well on the way to exploring the subtleties of up-down. In and out would come later.

I'd almost forgotten about the yo-yo man until I was called to the emergency room to see Maggie and listened to the history. It sounded as if he were back. Perhaps he had lost some of his enthusiasm, had become jaded by the commercialism in sports, the multimillion dollar contracts for hitting a ball or maybe just dropping one through a hoop. He had taken to wrapping up blocks of highway debris on a string and walking that dog along the side of the road, everyone going sixty-five in the fifty-five zone on I-90, even between a succession of local exits. He hadn't lost his proficiency. He could swing that concrete through a window as if he were trying to take the head off a driver. He almost did, damn near could have. Except Maggie must have seen something at the last moment. It was the last thing she would ever see, before both her eyes and the top of her forehead became unrecognizable. The trauma surgeon described it as a glancing blow, and she was still alive.

I took her to the operating room with the ENT surgeon. I quickly covered with surgical drapes the gaping wound where her eyes had been. I didn't want them watching me. The challenge lay in her opened forehead, and I sought to stop the bleeding. It was safe in there. I removed bone fragments from the brain and then sutured a patch in place, like Jorge's, to prevent a spinal fluid leak. The ENT surgeon removed remnants of tissue from her frontal sinus and then we closed the lacerated skin as best we could. I left the room as my colleague applied the dressing. I ignored what could have been a voice that came from underneath the drapes, as if her eyes were calling to me. "Come over and play. The Yo-yo man's here and Mace wants to take your picture."

PART FIVE

The Exit

CHARADE

If I rub my eyes it is not for want of shade from the South Florida sun that fills that reflective room at the top of the Heart Institute. It is more akin to a husband who has watched his haloed wife in her garden. But the image I wish to obliterate is that of Mace and his wide-set eyes that seems to call me to a place I have no wish to go. He would have me recite the third declension, "I am dying." I approach that lesson like a burning bush.

Not by studied contemplation, but by returning to the belly of what I do is required. No far-off ship on Government Cut or canopied floor of Sinai points the way. It is below in the floors of Judith's pavilion that the mystery of inevitable fate awaits me. There I am instructed by my predecessors to cast off the trappings of denial. It is no small task for a physician. Had we had our way, Margaret Clarke would not have been delivered from her beast by a final act of determination, but instead would have been devoured piece by piece as we doctors stood around. It would have been her more likely end, as she was relegated to a waiting room for the dying, a lounge perhaps, somewhere to sit among friends or family, even sojourners. While she reminisced or simply beheld whatever view was available, the battle would have raged without her. Sooner or later, all the patients are excused and Death and the doctors do their thing.

But there were exceptions that delivered me from this folly. At the end of a hall in a room decorated in the institutional fifties, sits a mother in a simple rocking chair, holding her dying son. Just as she was in 1971, in my first year of residency.

I must have known her name at the time, though I have divorced her from it now. She was never accompanied to that room by a husband or relative, some friend perhaps. It was as if she and her son had just appeared, migrant workers, to hell with child labor. The boy was dying of a brain tumor, though she appeared the stricken, toothless in her twenties and not from some rare disease. It was poverty that had robbed her of her youth. Her face had been ransacked by that scourge. Her lips were thin and her edentulous mouth pouted from within. Her eyes were dark and darker still, barely a lid between her brow and pupil. They had sunken in disuse. Her wonderment had ceased long ago, no smile or surprise could make those eyes laugh. She had nothing to hide and swept her thin hair above and behind her ears like a black headdressing. It was part of her training in neurosurgery, devoted to just one patient. Her wardrobe consisted of sleeveless blouses that made her arms seem more arthropod than woman. She had inherited her father's hands. They were broad, the fingers ringless, and they gathered her son to her with a workman's certainty. Yet for all those aesthetic sins, the image was of Whistler's Mother with a child.

As for the boy, he would have been a toddler if he could walk. But his world of motion had been limited to rocking. He was being taken on a journey not step by step, but back and forth. It was interrupted only by the intrusion of our assembly of house officers and a professor. Each day we would conspiratorially stop just before their threshold to review his chart. There were no letters of reprieve. As we entered the room our strides seemed inappropriately resolute. Perhaps we thought that death could be outnumbered. But the unbroken rhythm of the rocking and the mother's measured smile soon made us self-conscious. She had a forgiving countenance that conferred a different meaning upon our intrusion. It implied we must have been at play, perhaps inadvertently led into that room by a lost ball. We stumbled for the words to assert our presence. Certainly it was more than chance that had brought us there, all of us in white coats, presumably possessing the knowledge to restore her child to his child's life. Yet our powerlessness was absolute in the horrific devastation of his illness. We retreated into the technical, as was our custom in such awkward circumstances. We took note of the volume of fluids he had taken in and given back over the preceding twenty-four hours. We redefined success as to whether or not his anti-seizure medication had kept him still and we subjected him to a perfunctory exam, his frail arms compared in tone and strength. It was like examining a doll for the taking, except his taking was not ours and we had nothing left to give. We had already done what we could, two operations, Xray therapy, and still his tumor grew. It seemed to me a presence in that room and all three of them, mother, child and tumor, impatient with our charade. Why were we so insistent at this invasion of their privacy? It would have been better just to leave them to their rocking and waiting. They seemed content in their isolation, disrupted for reasons unclear even to ourselves. It was as if we were intimidated by that intimacy, put off by their apparent lack of concern for what we perceived as deadly serious.

We spoke among ourselves as if in another language, an aside. It was our competitive chorus of protest and denial. We reassured each other that we had fulfilled our obligations. Our leave-taking was awkward too. Any expression that the boy was holding his own or even a tad better would have been patently false. Instead we would suggest some aspect of observation or care to which the mother might attend. It was an effort to recruit her to our side, offered as much in jealousy as in anticipation of benefit. We had sensed that it was she who had intruded upon us. It was our hospital, our chosen form of disease, and our field of specialty to which we had staked preeminent rights. Her reliance upon that unproved and unorthodox remedy of rocking was depriving us of our full measure of care. There were procedures and policies for bed rest and in-travenous lines. Just because she had felt her son kick his awakening in the months before his birth was no reason to think she could return him to that place from which he had come. By asserting a mother's claim to the dying days of her child she was reneging on an unspoken pact and her smile was neither sought nor deserved.

There was noticeable relief when we could at last retreat to the corridor. We had survived for one more day our daily humiliation of impotence. I imagined that in our absence the three of them would ridicule our efforts, wonder at our collective naiveté. Our sophisticated, highly trained coterie might just as well have been outdoors enjoying some fresh air. We could have waved as we raked the fall leaves from the patch of grass just outside their window.

Eventually we collected ourselves and almost as a group sighed, "Where were we?" We turned to our other patients who were still able and willing to cooperate with our intentions.

In the end, she wore us down with that rocking. We came to understand that death was no longer the enemy. We would enter that room with the respect that was the mother and child's due, sometimes simply send an emissary to inquire of their needs. They had none. When the child died, it was appropriately at night. I imagined the mother appearing before the nurse, a single lamp illuminating that otherwise empty work station. "Dead," was all she would have whispered.

I still see that mother and her son in Judith's pavilion. I leave them undisturbed. With the passing of the years I have come to view them in a different light. The boy is sleeping his child's sleep with his face buried in his mother's arms. The back of his hairless scalp, the only respondent to his therapy, seems newborn.

PERSEVERANCE

It is the exception to be delivered twice by our mothers or in the end held harmless in their arms. More likely we conclude our uncertain times in the grasp of doctors, and they are armed with resolve. After the passive chastisement of being replaced by a rocker, I am myself anxious to return to the fray and so enter Max Bergman's room. He was the patient who reminded me of my father. It was obviously more than his age, seventy-two and counting, while my father's had forever stopped at eighty. They shared a physical resemblance. It started with the high, honest prominence of their cheeks, that bestowed a focus to their gaze less demanding than tolerant. Their foreheads were broad, and seemingly knowledgeable, suggesting how both had chosen to pursue the American dream — my father, through the practice of law, and Bergman, in the proficiency of business. Their noses were patrician, neither caricature nor stereotype, sufficient to invite assimilation. And their ears were endearing, just large enough to hint at the strictness of their early years.

There had been no question that Bergman needed surgery. The progression of his arthritis coupled with nerve root compression from a herniated disc had made walking for him all but impossible. Admittedly the risk of his surgery was increased because of his history of heart disease. But the notion that the most important statistic in life is length of years had undergone revision in Bergman's mind. To him a continued life of disabling pain was no life at all. After consultation with his wife and attorney-son he had chosen to face the increased risks of surgery. He had survived a heart attack one year earlier, why not a straightforward back operation now? If all went well he would be freed from the back and leg spasms that accompanied each of his guarded steps. Like Judith Halpern he reasonably thought the risks I presented to him were only remote possibilities, afflictions intended for some other patient.

I performed Bergman's surgery with the orthopedic surgeon who had operated on him some years before. The scar tissue from that previous surgery had encased the spinal nerve roots. I removed that adherent tissue with the laser as I would have Judith's tumor a year before, had it been benign. The surgery went well and the orthopedic surgeon closed the wound. I don't think that made any difference. The spinal fluid leak that appeared a day after surgery would most likely have occurred anyway. But it was a turning point in Bergman's care, an omen, that portended not only a failure of wound healing, but the possibility of a life-threatening infection as well. The fluid was arising from his body's biological spring which would not run dry. Unless diverted or contained, a procession of clear drops would continue to emerge along his suture line like prisoners from a tunnel.

The contest was clear: fluid draining from a wound in an amount sufficient to soak Bergman's dressings and sheets, pitted against my determination to keep that wound dry until healing could occur. But that could be as difficult to accomplish as parting the sea. I remembered the lost skirmishes I had waged with wounds draining spinal fluid in other patients. In some I had placed additional sutures only to see fluid appear a short distance away. In others I covered the wound with the thick dressings normally applied in abdominal surgery, hoping that in a darkened and protected environment cooler heads would prevail. Wishful thinking was just that. When I had peered under those ponderous dressings, drops of fluid seemed to scatter like insects exposed to a light. The presence of a leak did not go unnoticed by surrounding tissues. It caused the skin on either side of an incision to become raised with a sensitivity that might have occupied the patient's full attention were it not for an unremitting headache, aptly named "spinal" for its origin.

The application of principles relating to water management was what would be required, sophisticated plumbing to be exact. If Bergman's spinal fluid could be diverted inside his body, before it reached his wound, healing would occur. It was even possible he might be spared a second operation. I decided to perform a spinal tap in his room and insert through the spinal needle a catheter that could be left in place and connected to a sterile collecting system. It had worked in other patients.

I asked Bergman to lie on his side. A nurse helped him bend his knees to his chin. I tried to ignore the drops of fluid from his incision that seemed to be taunting me. It was euphemism time, "A little bee sting," I warned, as I injected Novocain above the grinning wound. Bee stings hurt, and Bergman, who reminded me of my father, had already suffered enough. His fetal position, on his side without a pillow, his knees and hips flexed, magnified what he was going through. As I punctured his skin with the sharp and beveled tip of the needle the spinal tap became a "blind" procedure, a progression of the senses. It required guiding the needle by feel and aim as Dr. Scott had done on Chemkowski and Graves. It wasn't blind in the sense that anyone walking down the hall might just as well have taken a stab at it. A knowledge of anatomy and experience were required, presumably what I was being paid for that day in Bergman's room. When the last membrane was penetrated, it would be betting time. Who would say that when I withdrew the stylet of that needle, spinal fluid would not follow close behind? That's if the procedure had gone well. But the needle met resistance, struck unyielding bone and glanced off the shingles that formed the roof of Bergman's spinal canal. Pleading, "Let me in" was not about to help. The spine was not about to admit every fool who showed up uninvited, hose in hand, with some breathless story about needing to drain fluid.

As the needle failed to advance through Bergman's spine as I had hoped, his procedure permit lay casually on the bedside tray. It documented a litany of risks that I had recited as a formality. It was only paper work that needed to be dispensed with before I could correct the factor that had occurred. Inserting the catheter was going to take care of his problem. It was well past the point of suggesting he could think about it. There wasn't any time for him to get back to me. The dam wouldn't hold much longer. Whether it was his arthritis that had narrowed the potential pathways for that needle, or just bad luck, the target seemed more imagined than real. The opening I sought became elusive, impenetrably walled. In my efforts the needle I was using, despite its adequate size and bore, became bent. Instead of being greeted by spinal fluid when I removed the stylet, blood from bone and muscle appeared at the open end of the needle. That wasn't the only sign of a lack of sympathy for the purpose at hand. There was bleeding as well from puncture sites on Bergman's back. They recorded the number of passes I had made in my ongoing efforts. It became personal then. Since in the past I had been more rewarded than chastened for perseverance, I chose to continue. I implored the nurse to keep Bergman from moving, suggested that if only she could cradle him in a true lateral position, at least do that right, all of this could be over. Then I dismissed Bergman, the patient who reminded me of my father, from my mind. It would be easier to continue with him out of the room. My attention was reduced to a patch of skin above recently placed sutures with swelling at its lower end and bleeding from several puncture sites; that and the son of a bitch fluid that needed to be diverted. A new needle became the extension of my resolve. The green towels which I had draped on his back slipped from their original rectangular placement. They had become skewed from Bergman's movements. I would have asked to have my brow wiped were it not for the fact that my ungowned forearm worked just fine. Only my gloved hands needed to be sterile. I pushed ahead because no one else was going to get that catheter in before Bergman contracted meningitis and died. Besides, what could go wrong?

At that moment, Bergman, who in reality was still there, who had been doing his best to remain in position, and who reminded me of my father, had an announcement to make. At the time what he said seemed more colloquial than foreboding, a little off the mark perhaps, but still within the boundaries with which I was familiar. I didn't think that only doctors should be permitted to stretch the language to their use. I didn't apply a literal translation to his faint pronouncement, "I'm dying."

Who could know it was the real thing? Patients don't die from spinal taps. He was exaggerating, referring to the fact that there was some pain. I knew that. It couldn't be helped. But there it was again.

"I'm dying."

"It's going to be OK," I replied in the tone and cadence of, "Eat your oatmeal."

I left out the aside, "Just remember who's in charge here." I knew I had to get that catheter in and that's just what I was going to do, even if it was to take all day. It was the same pledge that Dr. Wagner had made to remove Hampton's temporal bone, highlighted with the additional, "even if it kills me." Only this time the prophetic implications seemed less remote. The notion intruded itself in my mind that Bergman and I had ceased to be patient and doctor. I didn't want to define exactly what our new roles were.

There was a cacophony of distractions then. My thoughts seemed harder to dismiss. The nurses were talking among themselves about other patients. Who got what meds? What else needed to be done? And there was the barely audible, "I'm dying." It was almost an afterthought when instead of blood at the hub of the needle, I saw spinal fluid. My perseverance had paid off. I inserted the catheter, withdrew the needle from his back one last time, and secured the connection to the sterile drainage bag. I covered the puncture marks and catheter with a dressing. The wound was going to heal. There wouldn't be an infection. That's why I was the neurosurgeon and everybody else was everybody else.

It was time to invite Bergman and his doctor back into the room from wherever we had both been sent. If he looked a little pale it was not altogether unexpected, considering what he had been through, the draining wound, the headache, the tap. He would perk up after a little extra pain medication. Except that's not what happened. I was called by the floor nurse a few hours later. The patient in whom I had placed a spinal catheter was complaining of chest pain. The nurses had notified his cardiologist as well. A repeat electrocardiogram suggested acute changes. That was the way it was supposed to be in a hospital, heart attacks are not brushed off as indigestion. Bergman was transferred to the intensive care unit. I sought solace in profanity, "Son of a bitch." I weighed a phrase against a procedure, Bergman's, "I'm dying," compared to the need to insert a catheter into his spine.

I had thought until then, with one exception, that patients didn't know when they were dying. As for those who thought they were, we sure as hell tried not to let them. They could die in some other hospital on another doctor's service. Bergman didn't wait. He didn't say anything else, he just went flat line. They broke a few of his ribs giving him closed chest compressions, but nothing came back. Afterward, I spoke with his wife. We talked once more about the risks he had chosen to face. She remarked how it seemed his leg pain was gone after the operation, and how grateful they both had been. It was the consensus of the living. He was a seventy-two-year-old white male with a history of cardiac disease who had undergone spine surgery. It had gone well, no need for a blood transfusion, just a little spinal fluid coming from the wound. That was no problem. I would divert it into a sterile bag for a few days and the wound would heal without incident.

PATIENCE

I had initially attributed Bergman's prescience to theater. I assumed that what he meant to say, was, "Please stop." "I'm dying," was simply a more forceful effort, intended to convince a reasonable person, or one without a mission, that he could endure no more. I might have said the same thing had I been coaxed into a fetal position for what seemed like an eternity. Yet his tone had suggested neither indictment nor entreaty. I have come to think that perhaps he was witness to some last view of his own mortality. If so it inspired less fear than understanding. Held in that embryonic state, he may have been predisposed to a spiritual involution as well. As he lay cradled in the arms of a nurse-mother, perhaps he looked within himself and discovered his return. Nothing left to say then but, "I'm dying."

If that were true, perhaps I could believe that Anna Kwan had been similarly inspired. Just as Bergman remains fixed for me in a primal resting state, on his side with only a small portion of his back visible, Anna lies forever on a stretcher outside the arteriogram room, paralyzed and afraid, her life about to be taken from her because of what would be called a "stray bullet." She was parochial-Asian, no older than fifteen, her school uniform cut from her body in the emergency room after an endotracheal tube had been placed in her throat. That tube and the respirator were keeping her alive. Her breathing had stopped when the bullet had pierced her neck. A fragment of bone displaced by the impact had transected her spinal cord at a level above the nerves responsible for respiration. Her brother, at her side as she fell without a cry, breathed for her, his mouth to hers, for fourteen minutes until the ambulance arrived. His efforts had kept her not only alive but awake. She could blink her eyes in response to questions, once for yes and twice for no. There seemed no doubt, no doubt at all, that she understood that something terrible had happened to her.

I was the neurosurgical resident on trauma call.

"Can you feel me touching you?" I asked.

Two blinks.

"Are you in pain?"

Two blinks.

There was no movement of her arms or legs and all of her muscles seemed void of tone. She was unable to feel the sharp end of a safety pin. Successively stronger stabs, perhaps made to deny the completeness of her loss, trailed drops of blood along her abdomen to just below her neck. Her loss of sensation and movement were complete below the wound. It was an examination that suggested no chance for recovery. The plain Xrays told why. The bullet lay in its terribly incongruous position, embedded in the vertebral body of the third cervical segment. A fragment of bone occupied space meant only for her spinal cord. That was why little beyond blinking her eyelids and looking from side to side was preserved. Her ability to grimace was obscured by the tape used to anchor her endotracheal tube to the skin of her face. But when I requested, she could protrude her tongue a short distance beyond her lips.

All that, from what was called a stray bullet. It strained the concept of fate to think that only chance had led it to her neck. A malevolent force was more readily comprehensible. All that was required was a boy with a gun, flush with a gang at his side. That weapon had not been fired at its intended target, some other boy of some other gang almost a block away. The hand that held that pistol, and the arm that raised it were guided. A perverted mentor on that after-school street must have whispered, "That's right, just like this." And then, "Now."

Anna had fallen, her brother had kept his mouth to hers, and then I stood by her side in a corridor of the Xray department, waiting for her arteriogram to be done. We needed to visualize the major arteries in her neck. If one had been injured by the passage of the bullet, its wall could be weakened and subject to rupture. Within hours it might give way and her life end from a sudden and overwhelming loss of blood. There wasn't any concern about her brain. Her appropriate blinking demonstrated she was alert, although I hoped not fully oriented.

As I looked down at her I was struck with the hopelessness of ever reversing her neurologic damage. The neuroradiologist who was to perform the study stood by her side as well, waiting for the room and equipment to be declared ready. Phil Kim was short, clean-shaven and also Asian-American. If he or Anna felt a kinship, it was not apparent. Anna seemed lost in her child's innocence and in what I hoped was her ignorance of the enormity of what had befallen her. Kim seemed occupied by his review of the plain films and the technical aspects of what he would need to accomplish. I repeated her examination, hoping in that hallway, beyond reason and experience, that what I had first seen was only temporary. Rarely, a loss of spinal cord function could be secondary to concussive effects. In time, normal functioning of that exquisite structure might return. That was subject to its remaining intact and not competing for space with a fragment of bone. I partially uncovered the site on her abdomen where the safety pin had left its imprint of my frustration. Anna blinked twice to what was this time a non-blood-letting test of sensation. There was no movement when I asked, "Wiggle your toes for us." Almost as an afterthought, I asked, "Anna, stick out your tongue." I had meant it as a rein-forcement, hoping there might be a sense of comfort to her in performing the simple maneuver over which she still had mas-tery.

Despite what seemed to be a concentration reflected in her eyes, beyond one and then two blinks, there was no discernible movement of her tongue. Her lips did not part in the careless way that children project their teasing displeasure. Whether this last failure carried her over the edge of her childhood sanity or she unmistakably read the alarm in my eyes, she became un-done. It wasn't so much what she was doing with the muscles of her face, a grimace that enveloped her eyes with an ageless grief, it was what she was doing with those eyes. She blinked twice and twice again, a pause each time with an expertise in signaling as if she had been doing this all her life. Two blinks and again twice, two blinks like some titanic if not abbreviated SOS. At first I thought she might be seizing, a fatal hemorrhage from an injured artery triggering her brain to issue a general alarm. It would have been a call to stations which none of the other crew could have answered. It wasn't a seizure and her reaction was not disproportionate to her status. I had uninten-tionally uncovered evidence that the damage to her spinal cord was ascending. Her brain stem, the most inferior and primitive portion of her brain, the last section of the specimen cut by Dr. Mills, was being drawn in to that fatal shot. If the progress of spreading destruction continued, more than a loss of protruding her tongue was at stake. Her body's ability to sustain a blood pressure and manifest elemental consciousness would be lost. There wasn't a machine that could be wheeled in next to the ventilator to replace that. She seemed beyond reassurance, had I possesed the commitment to charade to offer it to her. If only she could have cried out in that corridor, while all around the routine science and commerce of that department passed us by. I sent the ER nurse who had accompanied us to radiology for sedation. Intravenous morphine was to be the antidote to the poison that had seized her soul.

All of that would have been enough, the stray bullet, the paralysis of her arms and legs, the inability to protrude her tongue which pronounced the final sentence, and yet there was more. Kim, standing on the opposite side of the stretcher, leaned over Anna as if to offer further explanation of the test she was about to undergo. Perhaps he was unaware of her deterioration. Before I could draw him aside he whispered, "Just be patient a little longer. A lot of people are staying beyond their normal shifts to try and help you. OK?"

It was his best effort, offered without a trace of malice or impatience. Yet the monstrous incongruity of his doctor-to-patient remark turned me from my purpose. Anna's life was ending. I saw it with the clarity of my own temporary state of grace. For I was still standing, defying gravity, free to move my arms and legs at will, swallow, feel the texture of the fabric of my clothes against my own skin, and still plan the future with the conceit of the unknowing. As for Anna, her plans for college and someday marriage, career and motherhood, the donning of clothes, all were lost. Yet Kim had suggested that the losing was ours, staying "after our shift," a largesse of dedication which he hoped she understood.

I remained silent, knowing that she was dying, suspecting she knew as much herself. I could just as well have been Lord Jim, over the side, the din of the breaking sea and the wind drowning out whatever I might have said, or what she might have wished me to say.

I could have taken Kim's arm, forcibly drawn him back to her side, and in that physical act become her proxy, better than a tongue.

"No, that's not right, he didn't mean that. The time is unimportant now. We're here with you and we're not going to leave."

I might have said that but I didn't, as if the handrails on her stretcher had become a barrier to her needs and my redemption.

"Be patient" had been Kim's advice, as the hourglass of her life spilled its last grains. Then whether from the exertion of her panic or as a sign of surrender, her struggling grew less. I withheld the morphine. She seemed to be looking beyond us, appropriately so was my thought, for all the help and comfort I had been. I wondered if she saw her life spilling away in that hourglass. When the uppermost chamber was filled with her future, it had invited contemplation, the full curvature of its abundance distorting inevitable loss. Now, almost empty, there would have been a clarity of detail, each individual grain seen as a moment of time and memory. Perhaps the running sand had given way to another image, something vast and almost unfathomable, becoming clearer through the unobstructed glass. I thought of Mills and the thickened jar which held a brain. He stood before the window that had overlooked the Thames once again. Then Anna's face suggested it made no difference which side of the railing or hourglass or window any of us were on.

Kim and the technician wheeled her away, took her into the cell-like angio room and closed the heavy lacquered door behind them. That door reminded me of my grade school. I wondered if Anna's school, the one she had left just a little more than two hours before, had doors like that and ponderous wall clocks inside, each between an American flag and a portrait of Lincoln. Those clocks would have told time not as an hourglass but as a calendar. It was fall and Anna was fifteen, a ninth grade student. The hands on those clocks would have seemed never to move.

Time hadn't stopped. Kim came out of the room twenty minutes later. The films were technically perfect, suitable for slides for his teaching file. The bullet that had somehow strayed into her spinal column had damaged one of the major arteries in her neck. But there was no danger of a weakened vessel wall giving way. All flow had stopped where the injury had occurred. In the irony of that futile afternoon, the films showed that Anna had been blessed with perfect collateral circulation. Her one remaining carotid artery was supplying blood to both sides of her brain. Had she lived it would have been another detail to the story that she would have told her children. In her softened version it would have been about how, when she was a little girl, she had hurt a blood vessel in her neck. God had given her other vessels so that it didn't matter. She would have told them that story at bedtime as they sat in her lap and ran their fingers over the barely rough edges of her scar, feeling the slight indentation of a healed puncture site, the entrance wound of a stray bullet.

Anna died before morning rounds. The brain stem swelling claimed all of her, not just her tongue. It was forever too late to speak to her of clocks or hourglasses, or about the shame and sorrow I felt, but did nothing about, when one of my own had asked her to be patient.

SUBSTITUTION

Resurrecting Anna's last hours never seems to place my memory of her entirely in perspective. Perhaps a school girl, paralyzed and dying for no other reason than that she was walking home, cannot be understood. Still there is a natural inclination to seek design in the otherwise random. Separate us from the trappings of myth and we might all go mad. From single cells to whales we must apportion purpose. I find Ahab misunderstood. Why shouldn't Moby Dick have assumed a malevolent presence? The captain's obsession has served us all. Bound by harpoon lines to a demonized whale is as satisfying an end as there is. Give us our myths. Jesus loves us. Allah is great. The Lord is one. Who wouldn't require that reassurance when forced to quit Anna's side, walk alone the distance between that forsaken corridor in Xray to the emergency room, the last outpost of Judith's pavilion? It is there, in that dying place, whether through punishment or penitence, that I share last rites with two contemporaries. One is a stranger, the other a friend, and it makes no difference.

The friend was Harris Pasline. From the time we were toddlers until his death, he was always a year older and a head taller than I. The backs of our houses faced each other across the interior of a residential block, filled with yards, detached garages, pullied clotheslines, and one gravel-covered alley. If we couldn't hear one another from our bedroom windows, we were still close enough to share the thrill of learning to ride our two-wheelers on that seemingly endless gravel path and later to exchange the furtive tales of puberty that fired our imaginations. It was impossible not to be his friend. Steadfast in the background of his mother's puritanical home, her commandments broadcast from windows at the least hint of apparent transgression, Harris wore his father's calm demeanor. The two of them rode the vocal storm of those unbreakable rules with the tolerant affection of Utah Watkin's berated farm animals in *Under Milk Wood*. Harris kept to his friendships with the predictability of milking time. As we pursued our individual careers, he refused to permit college or profession to come between us. Even after he married he maintained contact with his bachelor companions through calls and invitations. And then it stopped, the time all wrong, when he died on a July 4th afternoon, stricken by a heart attack at thirty-seven. I learned the details of his death gradually over the years from acquaintances whom I had never known as well as Harris, now made more familiar by our shared survival. If the story seemed fragmented in the barren painfulness of the telling, still I assembled in increments an image of how he had died.

Always the host, Harris and his wife had planned a holiday celebration. Friends and family were expected. Then, before noon, he had developed chest pain. It was somewhat more than could be attributed to a previous day's dietary indiscretions, more than a pulmonary catch left over from a cold. There was a heaviness to it, a pressure. He had his wife, Susan, drive him to the hospital. They pronounced him fit there, or at least as free from the definitive signs of a heart attack as could be documented, just in case. One version had it that he had been offered admission, overnight observation had been suggested. There was something selective about a thirty-seven-year-old attorney who presented himself to the emergency room complaining of chest pain. Better to be safe than sued. Whether he declined or it had never been offered, he and his wife went home. If they were secure in the knowledge that his electrocardiogram had been normal and his juvenile diabetes was under control, it wasn't enough to dispel their mutual understanding that Harris would rest for the remainder of the day. He would forego his preparations and remain in the upstairs bedroom until the guests arrived. "Found dead," was the common conclusion.

I should have gone to his funeral, can't remember now what surgery I might have performed that day. Instead I excused myself from a thousand miles away, the distance from Florida to Pennsylvania sufficient to invite regrets, even for a friend who could have been my brother. I wrote to his parents, my version of *A Note from Anne*. I tried to tell them that it seemed as if Harris had a special sense of time, knew it might not always be there, presaged his early death. Perhaps that was why he had insisted on keeping us all together. But I couldn't sign off on our friendship with just that note, or simply leave a rock on his stone after reading the dates of his shortened life each time I visited the cemetery where my father had been borne. What remained undone stayed within me, as if I had placed it in a briefcase, carried it to work each morning, had it in the car on the drive home.

I eventually forgot that need, if not Harris, until years later when I mistakenly opened the curtain to the cubicle of trauma 2. I had been called to the emergency room to see a patient with a head injury. Since the nurses were busy obtaining the vital signs of other patients, and the ER doctors were tied up suturing scalp lacerations, I decided to help myself. I'd find the patient they had asked me to see.

If trauma 2 was where my patient lay, I was obviously too late. The sheet-covered body told me that. I thought a more thorough investigation might inform me if my work were truly done. Yet no forty-year-old woman whose head had collided with a windshield lay beneath that sheet. Then, before I could look away, it struck me who it was, or who it just as well might have been. Harris, dead at thirty-seven, husband and friend.

The image was distinct, the smooth skin of the eyelids, the closely shaven face that could never erase its five o'clock shadow, the relative youth despite the premature gray hair. It could have been Harris in repose. That handsomeness was hardly common. Like Harris's, the heart of the patient before me should not have stopped. Someone had made a terrible mistake. In that error was the subject of my unrealized grief, a soliloquy that had yet to be delivered. I sat down on a metal stool by the side of that stranger and grieved for my lost friend, not because I was light-headed and had no choice — there was no distortion about the eyes, but because it was time. A nurse found us both, asked me if I were all right and explained this wasn't the patient they had wanted me to see. This was the man who had collapsed and died in a restaurant.

I had been about to give voice to Harris, as I would have wished him to do for me, were I nothing but a memory. Instead I chose to state the case for the stranger. Found it all the same. Turned around a Dylan Thomas poem, after the *last* death there are no others.

I might as well have tapped a spoon on an empty water glass as I stood to speak for the stranger in a now silent restau-

rant. There were no signs that a man had died at lunch. The tables had been reset, the linens and silverware made ready for
the evening's sittings. It made it difficult to begin.

What was there to say? That he had not known this might
one day happen? Loved ones go to work and school, even upstairs to rest before a party, never to be again. The death of one
man in a restaurant hardly needed justification, not in the
twentieth century when babies had been thrown into the fire
with their mothers and fathers on an industrialized scale.

Nor did I choose to rebuke his luncheon companions, simply because at first all of them had laughed. That's how he had
been taken, with friends and strangers nearby. Silverware,
plates and glasses, a wicker basket with warmed rolls, all had
been sent over the side, like a dining room trick gone terribly
wrong.

It was just that he had been allowed no time at all, not a
moment, a few seconds, to simply say good-bye. He could have
whispered a few words, what to tell his wife, or children. His
silence was made more barren by the continuation of life beyond his immediate table. There was laughter. Someone asked
for salt. At last there had been a respectful hush until he was
carried to the ambulance, minimal social expectations eventually had come in to play. But soon the gaiety returned. Someone
had said it seemed as if he had stirred just at the doorway in
that afternoon light. He was soon forgotten as if the embarrassed witnesses had been little more than worker ants, a bit
of German in all of them. They had kept about their business
while the Gestapo had grabbed one of their neighbors. It had
made little difference if he were a Jew or Catholic, a cripple of
some sort, so long as they were not the one, at least not this
time. Only his luncheon companions had the decency to disperse.

I thought that like Anna and Bergman, something beyond resignation had overcome him at the end. His thoughts would have been less of regret than recollection. Then he was walking the streets and listening to the sounds of a city, as sweet as a symphony. He eavesdropped on two old women waiting for a bus whose attention had been drawn to a boy passing by holding a skateboard. He noticed the way a leaf moved in the wind. There was almost a secret to it. Given enough time he was certain he could decipher its message.

The stranger ended up sitting on a curb just outside a restaurant, Harris kneeling by his side. He explained to Harris that he had just wanted to feel the cement, said there was a texture to it, how it seemed different depending on whether it was touched with the tips of the fingers or rubbed lightly with an open palm. He pointed to the rounded ledge and mentioned how he had always wanted to do something like that, work with his hands. Have a trowel, run it over the cement. Asked, "Did they begin with a frame?"

"That's probably how it's done," he reasoned.

"Start with the boards. I'd need the proper tools of course. Begin first thing in the morning, maybe even miss breakfast. Everybody else would be waiting for me to finish before they could do their thing, the bull work, mixing the cement, the smell of it on their hands. And when it was time for lunch, I'd eat what my wife had prepared for me, maybe just a cheese sandwich on dark bread. That's living, let me tell you. I wouldn't care about linen, or crystal glasses, never step a foot in a restaurant again. No need to."

Then the ambulance came. They put both of them in the back, the stranger still going on about that curb.

CELEBRATION

Like Harris and the stranger, I too am transported back to the emergency room of Judith's pavilion. If who I am is what I do, it is only right that I should be there, on duty on a Christmas night in Erie, called to see a patient who has shot himself in the head. His holiday gesture was genuine. The CAT scan and my examination reveal he has sustained an overwhelming injury to the brain. I make my way to the waiting room outside of the intensive care unit where his family has been escorted.

Old Erie is there, no recent emigrees resettled by virtue of corporate command or recruited within the professions. The father and daughter I have come upon are fourth generation outpost Pennsylvanians. When Horace Greeley suggested to young men that they go west, Erie could have been the place he had in mind. Those who heeded that call acquired a shoreline vigilance that the first namesake Eriez Indians may have had. Since Canada lay to the north of the Great Lake's gray waters, perhaps it was only natural to consider what might be coming from the other three directions as equally foreign. There wasn't a need for suspicion when assumption would do just as well. They knew what newcomers had been up to while they had been weathering winters without end. It was mentioned every Sunday in homilies about their Savior, and was part of the curriculum in their sectarian institutions of higher learning where dual appointments in the departments of Religion and Ethics stamped the certainty of their convictions. And they listened to the tales of their quiet money. That's what it's still called in Frontier, where stately homes guard the cliffs that rise along the city's most affluent shoreline. No Circle Line tourists or cruise passengers eye those mansions with covetous design. Perhaps that's why the money just whispers, barely loud enough to be heard above the crackling embers, repeating the details of insider contracts that might just as well have been concluded with a handshake.

Holly Gardner and her father were understated in that same way. Holly was bedecked in dark green velvet and muted red, a single white ribbon in her hair. She was in her early thirties, with brown shining hair and just a hint of holiday makeup. We had met before under different circumstances. She worked for a time as a public relations administrator at one of the hospitals. She was well chosen for her position. She had a natural way of talking that conferred a sense of well-being on her listeners. Of course whatever she said would make sense. Weren't her brown eyes wide with the honesty of her message? They laughed in their own right. And there was that diction again, traceable only to privilege. This night she sat with her father, Page Gardner, as if they had been called in from some affair of state. His white shirt was still buttoned at the collar. He had felt no need to loosen his seasonal tie. His gray hair was perfectly trimmed as if a corporate barber visited his office once a week. He had the distinguished air of Anglo-Saxon Protestantism that seemed to madden most democrats. Father and daughter's Christmas night gathering had abruptly ended with a call from the hospital.

"Is this the family of Clement Gardner?" the nurse had asked. "There's been an accident. Mr. Gardner's condition is quite serious. Perhaps you should come in."

They were the family, niece and brother, all that was left in Erie in the sense of immediate genes. If Peter Kosinski's trek across Dade County with his brother's Xrays spoke of the ties that bound in Miami, then Holly and her father's stiffly seated bearing had something additional to say about attachments among the city's old shore inhabitants. Perhaps it related to the ice that formed on the lake each winter. To the uninitiated it might have seemed possible to walk to Ontario. But the natives knew better. The brittle waves, frozen in their break, might be hollow underneath, give way to a fateful step. The frigid water underneath could stop the heart of a victim no matter how close or sure-handed were friends or relatives. *On your own,* was the reflection from that unending ice. Just as Clement Gardner had been, journeying who knows where, on a night remembered for a starlit trek.

It was only after Holly and her father had arrived in the emergency room that they were told what had happened — attempted suicide. They were allowed to see Clement then. A nurse had led them to trauma 3 and for some reason had left them unattended. Some of the debris of the initial resuscitation remained scattered about the stretcher and on the floor. They had seen a blood-stained square of gauze with a substance on it that they didn't recognize at first. Next to Clement's face, lying on the sheet, was a copper wire with a coil at one end. It had been used to support the tube that had been inserted in his trachea to protect his airway. The ventilator seemed to be standing guard, reaching down to him from its crane-like arm as if providing mechanical sustenance. His features were distorted, straining the experience of even medical personnel. It was the artist again. Only this time he had inserted among the images of mistletoe and turkey one of carnage. Clement's eyes were swollen shut, the thin skin about them discolored mostly blue with streaks of red. Trickles of blood, like tears, welled from beneath his eyelashes. Together with the bleeding from his nostrils and ears it gave him the appearance of a macabre marionette. Someone or something sought to manipulate him to the last. It was self-inflicted murder under a judgeless fluorescent light that Holly and her father had seen.

Clement was not yet dead. The cardiac monitor showed his heart was still beating. He had a detectable blood pressure, although in part from medication. When I had touched the surface of his eye with a wisp of cotton, there had been a slight flicker of his eyelid. There was the rub. That barely visible trace of movement was holding him on. Without it, he would have fulfilled the criteria of brain death. I could have broached the subject of organ donation. Instead, despite the awful destruction revealed by his skull Xray, metal and bone puzzled together on both sides of the brain, Clement still had some function. It meant nothing, nothing at all. No hospital or doctor could put him back together. At best, using a term that defied reason, he might be kept "alive" for an indefinite time. Were I to take him to the operating room and remove what I might euphemistically describe as devitalized brain, he might live, eventually perhaps regaining the ability to breathe. But he would not move purposefully, or speak, or understand speech. He would not react to his environment in any human sense. That's what I was prepared to tell the father and daughter waiting for further word about Clement. Suggest that nothing be done for the time being and let nature take its course.

I introduced myself. Holly acknowledged we had met before. I began to share what I knew. Clement had apparently shot himself in his garage. A policeman had told one of the nurses about the gun. They were surprised that it had fired. I didn't mention that. I was about to describe the extent of his injuries, what my examination and the Xrays and CAT scan suggested was a degree of damage that had destroyed the individual they had once known. That's when Holly held out a photograph to me. It was the gesture of a young child — if not preverbal, come to language so recently as to be granted permission for pantomime. I took it and sat down beside her and her father, co-opted in that instant to a different standard of communication. Had I not understood that prattle on behalf of a client was her forte, I might have asked if they could hear me, gone off in search of someone to sign. Instead I accepted her gesture immediately. She had offered me relief from my prescribed role. She had handed me an eight-by-ten, black-and-white portrait in a silver frame. It had brown backing with an angled stand as if it had been waiting on some richly polished table near a door. I looked at Clement in that photograph, staring past the camera with his arms folded. He seemed to be in his early fifties then. It would have been twenty years before. He was wearing a dark suit. His tie and hair were dark. The white handkerchief in his breast pocket was folded in two peaks. He wore glasses with wire frames, the lenses barely visible. His expression was one of continuing stewardship. Neither Holly nor I said anything. I studied that portrait and indulged my ruminations in the solitude she and her father had imposed upon that waiting room.

I saw Clement and the gun in his garage. He would have felt its presence as he came and went amidst the rhythms of raising his family. He had kept it hidden on a shelf used for odd storage, behind a half-empty container of motor oil and a box of weed killer. He had left it there, wrapped in a cloth with bullets in the chamber as if tempting one of fate's most basic admonitions, that about a loaded gun. Not the sort of thing one would expect from a man with a folded handkerchief in his breast pocket. Perhaps that's why it was there, the wrath of Calvinism next to the Chrysler. It would have kept his world in balance. His moral victory was to go on one day at a time leaving that gun untouched. Not that he would have thought about it every day. At least not until the children were grown and his wife had left him. That was a mystery for which I could offer no grounds. The man in the photograph would have no use for divorce. A disintegrating marriage would be beneath him. For how long had he glanced at that shelf less from habit than resolve, paused before going into the house as if he had forgotten something? He had no way of knowing if that gun would still fire. He had left it there untouched. Perhaps in the back of his mind it was like an insurance policy and now it was time to collect.

Clement was alone on a night noted for fellowship. He had refused enough family invitations, and failed to appear when he had reluctantly promised, that they were no longer forthcoming. He would not be missed for several days. It was the timing of all of his relationships now. The only noise in the house was the steady hum of the furnace. He checked to make sure he had turned off the stove, went into the garage and went right for that gun. It was waiting for him, as patient and loyal as anything he had ever known. He wished he had taken better care of it, periodically cleaned the barrel and oiled the springs and levers. He thought he would find it rusted to hell, thought it would have served him right. There was enough light from the kitchen for what he needed to see. The purple cloth could have been swaddling for a baby. He unwrapped the gun and wiped off the dust that had seeped through the cloth. The signs of neglect were less than he had expected. Maybe it would work. He tried to remember one last time why he had left it there. It tasted like oil. Damn, if the trigger still didn't depress.

Clement's neighbors had at that moment been entering their house after returning from church. They had heard what sounded like a shot and had seen a flash through Clement's garage window. They saw a light on in his kitchen. They thought it best to make sure everything was all right, understanding somehow that it wasn't. There was an odor. The man recognized it. He called Clement's name until his wife returned with a flashlight. They peered into the garage and saw a foot without a shoe. The man wouldn't remember how he had cut his hand breaking the glass to get that garage door open. He waited beside Clement as his wife called the police. Then they watched as he was taken away. "Still alive," was what they heard.

"Jesus Christ, on Christmas night."

If only they had asked him over for a drink.

When Clement first arrived in the emergency room, he was just John Doe, gunshot wound to the head. The paramedics were right, he did have a blood pressure.

"Look what's coming out of the wound," said one of the nurses.

Another nurse had found his wallet in the brown pants they had cut from him. She kept looking between the photograph on his driver's license and the man on the stretcher. She found Holly's father's name on a card, Page Gardner, then located his number in the phone book.

That's how we were all there looking at a man in a photograph. I didn't ask Holly why she had decided to bring it to the hospital. Perhaps it had seemed as natural a thing to do as when she had handed it to me. At last I returned it to her, taking care to keep the image face up. If I signaled a return to what were my painful duties, it was again proactively met. Her father stood and asked if he might have a word with me. It didn't seem to elicit a glance of resentment from Holly, some bristling disappointment that there was a need for man talk. She never looked up from the portrait. It was as if she and her father had rehearsed this part as well. I dutifully followed him to the windows that lined the far end of that otherwise empty room. I had accepted this role reversal as readily as I had reached for that silver frame. The lights of the decorated tree in a corner behind us were reflected in the glass. Only a few cars passed on the street below. One lone figure walked to the parking lot across the street.

Holly's father didn't look at me nor I at him. Eventually he began, speaking as if he were thinking aloud.

"I don't think it was his drinking," he began. "Parts of his life were as fastidious as when we were younger, both raising families. He stopped coming to the plant. Said when we sold off his division — they had made gauges for fuel tanks — there wasn't any reason to. Christmas night. We used to have wonderful celebrations. I remember his wife made rum cakes. The boys had a train set they added to each year. The tradition was to end the evening at their house."

I watched his reflection in the window, wondering what he was seeing in that night. He was touching the fingers of either hand as if searching for something he had been holding or trying to rediscover the feel of something he had lost. There was the smell of alcohol but he didn't seem intoxicated. He might have noticed me watching him.

"We saw him, you know. That was brain on the sheet. I know he can't be saved. He took a gun. Stuck it in his mouth. Buddy, that's what we called him. It seems like so long ago."

He paused and turned toward me.

"Too bad you can't put it back inside like it used to be."

I knew what he meant, felt he didn't expect a reply. I had lost sight of the figure in the parking lot, couldn't see if perhaps he had turned back to look at the hospital and saw two figures silhouetted in that waiting room window. Page spoke again, this time directly to me.

"Someone said he was found in the garage. I wonder if he had been looking for the crèche that his wife insisted he display every year? Right in the front lawn. One year I tripped over it. I had gone back to our house for something. There were donkeys, a statue of a baby, of course, and a little crib."

He was sizing their dimensions with his hands.

"I couldn't find all the pieces, bent down looking for them, but just seemed to knock more things over. Finally I went in and found Buddy. Told him what I had done. He walked me back to the door. I thought we were both going outside to set everything straight."

Page hesitated, the slightest trace of a smile softened his face. "Instead, Buddy turned out the porch lights. 'Don't tell Babs,' was what he had said. That was his wife. That was it. 'Don't tell Babs.' It was the funniest thing I ever heard him say. We laughed that night. That's the way Christmas used to be. Both of us, too much to drink, the crèche knocked over, our Lord nowhere to be seen. That was when we were still a family.

Wish we were back there now, a pitcher full of daiquiris. You'd be welcome too."

He leaned toward me conspiratorially, lowered his voice though I doubt Holly could hear what he was saying.

"Dead for three years."

Page was winding down. He had a look in his eyes as if he were back there. He and Buddy. He didn't need me any more, didn't turn as I walked away. I had my answer. Holly looked up from the photograph as I stood in front of her. We shook hands.

"He's not suffering," was all I said.

"Thank you," and she let go of my hand. The lights on the tree blinked. I skirted the empty wrapped boxes at its base, leaving Holly and her father alone again as I returned to Clement.

SEPARATION

By the time I returned to the side of Clement's stretcher, there was no longer a question of what should be done. While Holly and I had been studying a photograph and Page reminiscing about Christmas past, Clement had left, all but his heart. Brain death was the clinical state, no euphemism there. It was a next-to-the-last pronouncement. The cardiac monitor still showed a heart beat, even though Clement had no detectable blood pressure. The see-saw that he had ridden for seventy-two years, one number on top of another, had stopped. The silver jointed arms that supported the ventilator tube were positioned above his face like a mobile intended for before-sleep amusement. Were it not for his attachment to a machine the green trace of what remained of his heart would have signed his undeflected end. Instead it was still there, that peg-leg march continuing across an indifferent monitor. I separated the plastic tube that had been inserted in his trachea from the ridged hose of the ventilator. A small pool of clear fluid, condensation from humidified mist, gently rocked in that hose. I held my hand over the opened end of the tube as I had done with Judith, more from habit than necessity. I felt nothing move as the second hand of what for me still meant time swept away the last contractions of his heart. The rate began to slow and, as with the boy whose disrupted eye had undone my vision, and the patient upon whom Dr. Scott had inscribed a tear, the difference between Clement and myself seemed to vanish. It was as if I were dying. I became the patient lying on a stretcher with a diagonal of tubes above me. An aboriginal tribal chief might just as well have appeared before me and pointed his stick of doom, and I, a believing victim, left no choice but to lie down and remain motionless until my heart stopped beating.

I heard my own voice then, and like Bergman's the message was, "I'm dying." The words were mine, though they had silently left my lips, which like Anna's had not moved. It seemed they had been whispered in a moment I could not remember, more to affirm than announce. Not, "You're dying," as if to trigger remorse or panic, some last survival instinct to sound a general alarm, but, "I'm dying," a pronouncement, a moment of benediction. The exclamation seemed primal, like first man in the garden. The power of the phrase resided in the words, "I am." It was a last possession, perhaps what had been revealed to Anna and to Bergman, and from them to me. It was transcendent beyond despair.

Scenes of my past returned to me then as a catalog of places and people. They appeared in my mind as if projected upon a screen like the candid photographs flashed in summary of the year's passing at my daughters' Erie day school's final assembly. I was drawn back into those moments however briefly, and thought to myself, this is what is meant by seeing your life flash before you.

I saw David and his mother. I had sat with them in the kitchen of their home. He and I were in second grade. His mother had come home from work with a small paper bag.

"I have a surprise for you, David."

In the bag was a single apple. Red Delicious was the variety I now know it to be. Then it was just an apple. She had brought a plate and a knife and ceremoniously carved that single piece of fruit as if it were the entree at a banquet. David watched, and I watched him. In our house of plenty, I had not seen this before. When his mother had finished, the apple was like a flower, each wedge a petal, and then she passed the plate first to me. Each bite I watched them take seemed steeped in a hushed appreciation that has stayed with me for forty years. He was there again, with his thin arms and small face, his teeth that seem early in decay, and the sounds he made as he bit into that apple.

A residential intersection was next. I heard the sound of tires, a horn, metal and breaking glass. It was the corner of West Lafayette and McCartney. A stop sign favored the level straight away that ran east-west, sought to halt the downhill momentum of the southbound traffic. By the time Harris and I reached that corner, the occupants of two cars stood in the street by the wreckage of that eventful night. It was summer evening, before air-conditioning hot, and yet a young girl, her father's arm around her, was holding a sweater to her forehead. She wasn't crying. Her father half guided, half carried her to the curb next to where we watched. Her brown hair was straight and reflected the streetlight under which she sat with a radiance that shone from all but one side, the side where she held the sweater. An ambulance arrived a few moments later, and someone placed a towel around the girl's head, almost like a dressing. A few drops of blood had fallen to the street and stained the macadam with uncertain borders. A neighbor whom I did not know had retrieved the sweater as the girl was helped inside and driven away. On the brown wool I saw the darker stains of her bleeding and a pattern of reindeer that danced across that makeshift bandage.

There was a photograph of Sheila Nolan. It was spring-posed and tree shaded, the single blade of grass that she held as textured as her red hair. And then other faces returned to me with their names, Ricky Bullette who had no fear at shortstop, Billie Danjczek, whose brother was kept watchful on a clothes-line, Mimi and Karen and Leah.

Then the subjects seemed less random, had a certain theme about them. How I might not have even made it that far, standing by the side of a dying man on a Christmas night, waiting for his heart to stop. I was on my bicycle again, hurling from an alley, unseen by the driver of a car until it was almost too late. He stopped in time and I saw again pure anguish in his face, not directed towards me, but at how close he had come to ending a life.

A scene from a birthday party appeared. There were sirened streamers on strings flying another year's passing. I boasted to Phillip Mitman (it was his father's grandfather clock that had been in the family for over two hundred years) to "watch this time job." As if in slow motion I sailed a streamer across the path of an oncoming car, timed it perfectly, so that the red bunting lay across the windshield at eye level as if there were a weekend sales bonanza and they were giving away bal-loons. The driver was good. He braked and pulled to the curb. There wasn't the sense about him though of impersonal an-guish. It was more like rage and a desire to catch whoever had thrown that streamer on his windshield. That was why I shouldn't have been standing by that stretcher with Clement already gone. I had darted across that street as if it were an open field. Only blind luck, turned around on my birthday, had kept a car from my path, just one block below the intersection where a girl with a blood-soaked reindeer sweater had sat on a curb until an ambulance came.

I refocused then, saw Clement below me, the man in the portrait who had been the master of his fate. His exit wound offered final proof of that resolve. Then the subliminal weight of what I had seen, from Hampton's surgery to Anna's suffering, and all that was between and since, seemed lifted from me. The paradox of neurosurgery had become inescapably evident. Not to have seen it would have meant one wasn't paying attention, as Buccheit used to say. In a specialty of the unwell, there were glaringly few who had reasoned their way out the window or to the wrong end of their own gun. Instead the natural conclusion was to be taken with one's own luck, the coordination of limbs, the preservation of speech, the elemental consciousness of, "I am." That's what came from standing by the side of a schoolgirl as she lay dying, and above a man who had shot himself alone in a garage.

Time passed and Clement died again. I returned to the nurses' station. There was a lull in the onslaught of holiday patients. The nurses and doctors were talking about their plans for the morning. They asked what mine were, drew me into their winter solstice celebration with the ease of our surviving brotherhood.

SURVIVAL

The waiting room was empty when I returned to tell Holly and her father what they already knew. I don't know why they had changed the rules. After all I was the doctor. They should have been overwhelmed by what they had seen and been told. My role was to help them make sense of what had happened, reduce to clinically manageable terms the imminent death of a close relative, one who lived in the same city and with whom they had evidently shared much in the past. First-line clergyman was what was called for, before a priest or minister appeared bearing the community's support. This was something more personal than what would have been drilled into them by ritual. This was death at the door, in the garage and behind the curtain. Death come calling on kin, genetic identity high enough to set off alarms at the cellular level. Reason and order, solace and purpose would come later. This was to help them keep standing, or sitting straight, not feeling a sympathetic headache that might turn to panic. That is, if they had needed it and had looked to me to explain why Clement was gone.

I was prepared for what was required of me. It was what I had done on holidays and non-holidays alike. I had been in the emergency room when a child had been struck by a car just after stepping from the school bus as her mother watched from across the street. I was on duty when a college student driving to her own engagement party was made forever late by a drunk driver. The teenager shot in the head when a gun went off at a New Year's Eve party, the boy who collapsed in the throes of an impromptu wrestling match, the wife who had been helping her husband work on their van when it slipped off the jack; all of them had relatives, survivors to whom I had talked.

I had been emissary from the land of injury and death dispatched to impose formality on nightmare, sent to rooms off of rooms, appropriately windowless, where the soon-to-be-survivors were escorted. These rooms are kept locked. They are not there for the social privacy of insiders, frequent visitors to the emergency room or intensive care unit. It would be unseemly if new initiates were asked to wait while a relaxed company of strangers was invited to quit the place. Their territorial stake, begrudgingly relinquished, would leave memories, like the bags of snack food and soda cans they would leave behind. Their we-were-here-first glances would be ignorant and maddening, justifiably inspiring a response.

"That's our Johnny in there you sons of bitches." Not the kind of enmity that can be easily dispelled.

Off limits, as they are, there is an aura that surrounds these rooms, an unspoken dread seen in the watchful eyes of the more fortunate. The nurses become warders; family members, waiting to hear the worst, their charges. These rooms are kept immaculate, the furniture simple and wall paintings eclectic. It doesn't matter what the subject. A Homer-tossed ship at sea is no less memorable than a reproduction of Van Gogh's flowers.

Each will be studied with the fervent hope of art, "Help me quit this place." They are the only rooms in which imposed claustrophobia is architecturally justified. Take these souls as remote from each other as the most distant stars and somehow fuse them. They are bereft, about to learn that a son or daughter, a husband or wife, someone who only hours before was part of them, is dying and beyond help. And why? What had they done that this should be visited upon them? However small or crowded these rooms, there is always enough space for one more. It is the apparition of the dying, well when last seen. If a child, don't get up. The corner will be fine. Knees to chin and those tiny arms folded in front, what wouldn't we give to have her here? An exchange? No dearth of volunteers to take her place where the doctors and nurses are with her now. "I've lived enough," in the minds of parents and grandparents. "Take me instead."

The couches are deep, though never deep enough. Let me sink further. The weight of my own body is oppressive while I am well and she is dying. All this, the silent child, the offerings, the physical transformations, why shouldn't these rooms have been waiting for such moments? They are like monuments, these rooms, that overwhelm the casual with their message. They impose on the bewildered a sense of what is to come. It is all timing. My entrance requires some delay before I can make any pronouncement, no matter how obvious and undeniable the loss. For it wouldn't do to take a quick glance at a patient and seek out the parents or spouse only to say, "It's no use." I will not be pawnbroker to bereaved and frightened relatives waiting for word of their treasures. My expertise is not some jeweler's loupe with which I can detect fatal flaws and casually offer inadequate compensation. The patients I have found beyond hope were growing children and loving spouses only hours before.

The younger the patient, the more crowded the room. Clement would not have been a big draw. Strike down a twelve-year-old, no matter what the date, and the motivation to come to the hospital to support her parents will be irresistible. We're all on call when it's a child. Those who have come are organized like a cast, with the closest of kin most accessible. It's always the same play with no shortage of available parts. There are supporting roles in the truest sense, friends who by their physical proximity and distracting speech signal that time and life still pass. There may be one hysteric whose sobbing, like public flagellation, gives vent to the common need. The quietly weeping serve their purpose too, like a brook that flows and carries with it pain and more pain. There, in the far corner, a silent one is positioned, symbolic of denial. In lieu of clergy there are believers. It is a time for Kaddish and to praise Jesus and Allah, recitative meant as enigmatic babble that speaks to our phonetic sense. We would fly to treetops from which we have descended. Comfort to the inconsolable must be dispensed. And who will ask the questions? Who will be the source of strength? A husband or father, unshakable in the past, may be unavailable now. Gone to pieces. May never be put back together. It's allowed in this room, disintegration.

Perhaps the white coat inspires silence. Introductions are kept to a minimum. I am the doctor, a neurosurgeon, and they must be the next of kin and others. This can be Shakespeare, unashamed. I am a seasoned performer who has played this part before, familiar with the demands of the material. My bearing is more than messagerial. Negotiations with death itself have taken place, no matter how one-sided.

To begin, there is the task of defining perspective, to place in context what has happened. Was it simply a question of too fast for conditions, trauma waiting by the side of the road to hitch a last ride? "Ejected from the vehicle," can say a lot. A child who has collapsed at a party is more problematic. There's not likely to be anecdotal prelude to that, some neighbor or friend similarly stricken.

Having recreated the unimaginable circumstances that have conspired to end a life I offer a statement of resolution. I have found none more telling than that attributed to President Kennedy's neurosurgeon. "The President demonstrated no signs of survivability." No signs of survivability, now there is a euphemism, the onus shifted from the living to the dying. Show us a sign, our son or wife, any sign. The least hint of sensation about the eye and we would mount an effort without limits to bring you back. Spare nothing would be our guide, surgery, machines and drugs, nightly vigils at the bedside with nurses at your pulse, if you would but show us a sign. Come back, come back. It is we who have been abandoned, left without a sign, though we have looked.

If you would but breathe. Is that too much to ask? That with the ventilator disconnected from that tube in your throat, with the slightest heave of your chest you reach out to gasp at life? Or move, to pin or pressure, fist upon breastbone eliciting a turn or grimace, a signal of enough. That you cannot see, seems irrefutable. The light is as darkness. Your eyes are wide and still and will not change. No signs of survivability.

It is another interval of time, this from word to thought. For just an instant there is hope preserved. Enough time for each word to be placed in context, side by side, and then the whole examined.

"No evidence of survivability."

"Then that must mean . . ."

"Yes."

It is that delay between phrase and meaning that becomes fixed, becomes part of this room. Relived how many times? A thousand? A thousand-thousand? Enough for the delay to become cumulative, enough for an appropriate good-bye, what they would have wished to say to child or spouse had they but known a last good-bye was upon them. Who would let go then, find the words of self? Had I said at first, "There's no hope," or used the term "brain death," the link between phrase and result would have closed instantly. Why not stay the inevitable for just a while longer? It's not a matter of intelligence or sophistication. It's not some perverted riddle that would mock the vulnerability of the bereaved. It is only words, a man in a white coat who's come to tell them that their baby is gone. "Not a piece of wood," as Dr. Scott would say. "There's feelings inside."

There's very little after that. "Not suffering," is offered but almost half-heartedly. The suffering is here in this room, more than enough to go around, enough to seep outside, fill each cubicle in the emergency room and then the halls and elevator shafts, the patient floors and radiology, the cafeteria and the morgue. It can't be contained, this suffering. It has stained these rooms, the furniture and walls. I depart, for a time to return. They leave, but are never gone.

ACKNOWLEDGMENTS

Thanks to Emily, Caroline, and Samantha for allowing Dad to write. To Richard Fitzgibbons and Kathy Havens, two friends who have for many years encouraged me to do so. To Harry Stauffer and Gail Cilladi whose dedication to their work allowed me to do mine. To Dr. Lamar Neal, Mel Snyder, Larry Dombrowski, James Graves, Charlie Miodus, Dr. William Esper, Dr. Alexander Kosenko, and Robert Ferrando Sr. who so graciously responded to my inquiries. To Elliot Harris for his legal presence, to Jeff Pinski for my first nod as a professional writer. To my copy editor Karen Gillum, who so patiently helped me let go, and to Suzanne Shepherd and Chip Fleischer at Steerforth Press, who transformed a dream into this tangible volume. To Jean Marc and Dafna Baier, who weekly attended the birth of my labor, and to Alice, who is the first and last of all my endeavors.

MARC FLITTER, M.D., is chief of the Division of Neurological Surgery at Erie, Pennsylvania's, Hamot Medical Center. He lives in Waterford, Pennsylvania, with his wife, Alice, and has three daughters. *Judith's Pavilion* is his first book.